California Cottages

INTERIOR DESIGN, ARCHITECTURE & STYLE

BY DIANE DORRANS SAEKS

PHOTOGRAPHY BY ALAN WEINTRAUB

CHRONICLE BOOKS

SAN FRANCISCO

Printed in Hong Kong.

Book and Cover Design:
Michael Manwaring & Elizabeth Ives Manwaring,
The Office of Michael Manwaring

Library of Congress Cataloging-in-Publication Data available.

ISBN: 0-8118-1137-9

Distributed in Canada by Raincoast Books,
8680 Cambie Street
Vancouver, B.C., V6P 6M9

10 9 8 7 6 5 4 3 2 1

Chronicle Books
275 Fifth Sreet
San Francisco, CA 94103

In the hills of Northern California: In his Sonoma cottage, San Francisco designer Orlando Diaz-Azcuy believes in sophistication and simplicity.

On the Cover:
A window on the natural world: California cottages are surrounded by flourishing trees and the bounty of nature year-round. Nick Mein and Jeffrey Doney found the wasp's nest at Lake Tahoe and display it in their Woodside studio.

Page 1:
Afternoon enchantment in Big Sur: Late in the day, golden sunlight gleams on the stucco walls of Kipp and Sherna Stewart's coastal cottage. The painting is by Kipp, a passionate watercolorist.

Page 2:
Theadora Van Runkle's canyon cottage feels far from freeways and care. Her orchid- and fern-filled paradise is just a few minutes drive from Sunset Boulevard and the glitzy boutiques and cafes of Sunset Plaza.

Opposite: Roses for the madonna: the graceful mise-en-scène in the living room of Tom and Linda Scheibal in the Napa Valley.

To My Son, Justin, and G.R.D. With Love—Always, D.D.S.

For My Mother and Father, Aunt Barbara and Karen—A.W.

Heartfelt Thanks to Everyone Who Helped
With *California Cottages*
— D.D.S. & A.W.

Contents

INTRODUCTION 9

City 13

Pale Perfection
THEADORA VAN RUNKLE'S COTTAGE IN LAUREL CANYON 15

Good Vibrations
ANDY & SHARON GILLIN'S HOUSE IN THE EAST BAY HILLS 23

Evocative Style
ODOM & KATE STAMPS'S HOUSE IN LOS ANGELES 29

Arts & Crafts
DR. DAN SIEDLER'S COTTAGE ON RUSSIAN HILL 35

Romantic Aura
ELIZABETH IVES MANWARING & TIM PERKS'S COTTAGE IN SAN FRANCISCO 41

Studied Simplicity
ELEANOR & NORMAN MOSCOW'S HOUSE IN THE CLAREMONT 47

Facing East
CEVAN FORRISTT'S FARMHOUSE IN SAN JOSE 55

Worldly Possessions
ALICE ERB'S BUNGALOW IN OAKLAND 61

Country Style 69

The Collectors
NICK MEIN & JEFFREY DONEY'S COTTAGE IN WOODSIDE 71

Civilized Seclusion
ISDA FUNARI & TONY MELENDREZ'S HOUSE IN THE SANTA CRUZ MOUNTAINS 79

Peace & Harmony
CARRIE GLENN'S COTTAGE IN NORTH BERKELEY 87

Family Legacy
JESSICA PARISH'S HOUSE IN MILL VALLEY 93

A Collector's House
HELIE ROBERTSON'S COTTAGE IN SAN ANSELMO 97

Country Colors
ORLANDO DIAZ-AZCUY'S HOUSE IN FREESTONE 101

Coast 107

A Poetic Place
SHERNA & KIPP STEWART'S BIG SUR AERIE 109

Cultivating His Garden
TIMOTHY MAXSON'S COTTAGE ON A HILLSIDE IN BOLINAS 113

Open to the Ocean
ED & KATHLEEN ANDERSON'S HOUSE AT SEA RANCH 117

Seascapes
CORINNE WILEY'S HOUSE ON BELVEDERE COVE 119

Sea Change
JOHN DAVIS'S HOUSE AT STINSON BEACH 125

Wine Country 127

Sunny Delight
JEAN & CHARLES THOMPSON'S WEEKEND HOUSE IN SONOMA 129

Memories of Majorca
RON MANN & LOUISE LA PALME MANN'S GARDEN IN SONOMA 137

Summer Bliss
RICHARD CRISMAN & JEFF BROCK'S RETREAT IN YOUNTVILLE 143

Living Among the Trees
TOM & LINDA SCHEIBAL'S LOG HOUSE IN ST. HELENA 151

Weekend Retreat
JO SCHUMAN SILVER'S COTTAGE IN SONOMA 159

CALIFORNIA CATALOGUE: DESIGN AND STYLE OF THE STATE 168

INDEX 175

Introduction

BY DIANE DORRANS SAEKS

I set out to find the best California cottages—and discovered something much deeper than decor, architecture, paint colors, and furnishings.

♦ I found people living in harmony with the landscape. I came upon passionate collectors whose lives were enriched by old books and new

paintings, folk arts, heirloom furniture, and treasure troves from flea markets and trips around the world. I discovered houses that honor the land and

build on the noble traditions of California architecture and design. ♦ Researching and photographing the houses in this book,

I looked for authenticity—never theme designs. One-note design, or decor that looks as if it all arrived on a truck on the same day, are not concepts

I admire or encourage, and they are not to be found in these pages. ♦ I sought out fascinating people—gardeners, and designers of furniture, cos-

tumes, textiles, graphics, and fashion, along with music lovers, architects, flower stylists, art dealers, executives, travelers, and a theater

producer—because the most individual and memorable houses are produced by people with singular tastes and unerring devotion to their own truth.

They are often irreverent, anarchistic designers who reject the idea of a nameable style, and thus move the idea of "good design" or

"good taste" into new realms. ♦ I grew up in New Zealand and have roamed the world ever since, so I hold great affection for those who make

building and designing a house a kind of exploration—of the world and of themselves. They voyage into unknown territory, with fabrics

and paintings and bricks and mortar as their passports. ♦ Since clear skies are rather regular occurrences in California, most of these houses are

also outward-bound rather than inward-looking. Doors and windows stay open most days, nature is ever-present, and the inhabitants

seem always on the verge of stepping outdoors to be greeted by perpetual sunshine. ♦ Many of these houses were absolutely willed back into life.

Timothy Maxson's studio on a hillside near Bolinas has a sunny disposition year-round.
Fitted with French doors and a redwood deck, it faces the ocean and is filled with sunlight from
late morning until the sun drops below the horizon. It's sheltered by a hardy stand of old
eucalyptus. A path of river stones meanders up the hill past flourishing mounds of lavender and
waving stands of flax. The bronze weather vane was a gift from his partner, Don Smith.

Carrie Glenn, who thrills guests at Chez Panisse with her extraordinary flowers and fruited branches, rescued a tumbledown cottage on the verge of collapse. Ron Mann propped up a leaning-tower-of-sticks tractor barn and turned it into an agreeable studio. Elizabeth Manwaring and Tim Perks polished a tiny rose garden cottage until it gleamed. Eleanor Moscow nurtured a venerable lodge mocked by a sixties commune. ♦ These are not showhouses built to impress. Someone who is intent on putting together a sanctuary and a retreat from the world, chair by esoteric chair, is not looking over their shoulder for approval, nor for social status through decoration. These renovators and designers dodge trends and celebrate familiar things, often imperfect and certainly showing signs of age. ♦ As Berkeley architect and visionary Christopher Alexander said in his seminal book *A Pattern Language* (New York: Oxford University Press, 1977), "Do not be tricked into believing that modern decor must be 'slick' or 'psychedelic' or 'natural' or anything else that current tastemakers claim. It is most beautiful when it comes straight from your life—the things you care for, the things that tell your story." ♦ When I first started discussing the idea of California cottages with architects and design chums, everyone had a fervent opinion about what archetypal cottages in California would look like. Several insisted that at heart they would be funky, woodsy, and rustic. Other soothsayers envisioned beach houses, open doors, and palm trees twirling like swizzle sticks beside the Pacific Ocean. Redwoods and adobe figured into some undercooked notions, along with cranky cottages up the North Coast, all woodsmoke and squinty eyes and chilled fingers. ♦ The truth is that California cottages are sometimes redwood-clad or sea-wracked, but they come in the widest possible range of styles, attitudes, approaches, circumstances, histories, provenances, and sizes. ♦ Some have been built on glorious land shaded by oaks that have breathed life into the landscape for centuries. Others have been rescued from desuetude, pulled from the maws of death, hammered and sawed and nailed and buffed into something worthy. Some of the sweetest survive in the city against all odds, still acting as if horses and carriages and railroads were daily conveyances. ♦ The approaches to renovation that worked best were referential—and somewhat reverential. If a house was changed drastically, it was to take it back to when it had been its best. The plan was to give it integrity, structure, and form, never to "modernize." The best remakes, like Isda Funari's reticent revival of a log cabin, are a triumph of style as well as common sense. ♦ In just the same way that a basic chair is very difficult to design, a room meant for living in, rather than merely looking at, is always a challenge. It takes confidence to make a personal room for day-to-day events and reject design by rote. ♦ Noticeably absent here is a riot of pattern. Those who trust their own taste and have a good, experienced eye for collecting and displaying antiques, seashells, children's paintings, framed prints, sculpture, photography, or meadow flowers, tend not to rely on patterned fabrics or printed wallpapers as the starting point for their rooms. When pattern is the main effect, all too often the draperies or sofa are pegged to a season, a year, when that print was in vogue. The houses presented here are aiming for a more subtle, lasting tonality. ♦ No one style works for everyone, and none of the houses here is a blueprint for "cottage style." Some owners handled the interiors as if they were of spectacular proportions, others took delicate steps. ♦ Lasting impressions are of a wasp's nest hanging on a wall, a burst of just-gathered 'Cécile Brunner' roses in a Mexican vase, light glinting through a cobwebbed window onto seashells, crunchy heirloom linens, lavender and rough stones, higgledy-piggledy books, and a rumpled pillow on a jasmine-shaded verandah. ♦ California cottages are full of living. They reflect early mornings at flea markets, hours spent reading and chatting, and a great commitment to the comfort of their rooms. The people who dwell there seem to have discovered some of the secrets of rooms. The people who dwell there seem to have discovered some of the secrets of contentment. ♦ The lessons from California's finest cottages are clear. Build or design a house in a borrowed country style without embracing its substance, and you risk creating a house that is all surface gesture, without heart. ♦ Ground the house in honesty, sincerity, and passion, and complete it patiently, and your home may come to touch the eternal.

Cottages in the city are just the ticket for those who want to be in the middle of things—but dwell in Arcadia. ◆ Theadora Van Runkle, who designs costumes for movie stars by day, lives in a dream of a house, high and flighty in the far reaches of a canyon. There she dreamed up a literary salon, a perfectly pale house in thirty shades of vaporous white. Isak Dinesen was her inspiration—along with sunstruck Roman afternoons, a rapturous Paris spring, and poetic Swedish country manors. ◆ And since this is California, the crosscurrents of influences keep coming. ◆ Interior designer and antiques dealer Eleanor Moscow grew up in Philadelphia and later transported the strict sobriety and craft traditions of Maine cottages to her sunny Berkeley home. Taking her lodge-style house back to its idyllic past, she polished up the ribbon mahogany floors, painted the walls white, and installed ticking-striped sofas and easygoing chairs. ◆ Kate and Odom Stamps, surrounded by freeways and urban noise in Los Angeles, swoon at the sight of understated English chintzes and gracious chairs that bespeak gentility. Their chic house is a recipe for living with a lifetime of collections, and devising interiors that are as personal as a signature. ◆ Cevan Forristt, adventurer and plantsman, journeys to Burma and Cambodia where he embraces the everyday things of those cultures. His engagingly eccentric old farmhouse, within walking distance of the glassy-eyed boxes of downtown San Jose, is like a postcard from some far-off country. ◆ Sharon Gillin and Stephen Shubel gave a sweet Eastlake Victorian a vivid new personality. Red-and-white-striped chairs, French antiques, and butter-yellow walls were just the beginning. ◆ These are all houses with somewhat brief histories. California is a young state, so they are no more than 70 or 100 or so years old, they are not world-weary but optimistic, adaptable, welcoming, and fresh.

A curvaceous buffet, an old urn, even frames, were given the white treatment.
Theadora Van Runkle painted most of the watercolors and oils on her
walls. She frames them with antique frames and moves them from room to room
so that they don't become "invisible." Van Runkle not only paints ravishing
renditions of the stars she dresses—she also draws from life.

THEADORA VAN RUNKLE'S COTTAGE IN LAUREL CANYON

Hollywood costume designer Theadora Van Runkle can hardly remember a time when she didn't live in her house at the top of Laurel Canyon. She purchased the cottage almost 30 years ago, and has lived under its spell ever since—except when she has been away in London, Rome, New York, or Paris, dressing the likes of Faye Dunaway, Jessica Lange, Demi Moore, and Liam Neeson. ◆ The gray-green clapboard residence stands half-hidden by elms, tangles of jasmine, banks of old begonias and rampant ivy, far from the over-heated, brightly lit valley below. ◆ Van Runkle can see the legendary "HOLLYWOOD" sign in the distance from her front porch, but the house makes hardly a nod to Tinseltown. Originally somewhat dark, with Victorian furniture cloaked in dark velvet, it later went through a Greene and Greene and William Morris period, and more recently, a lighthearted flowery phase. Today, the cottage is dressed in its new finery—all creamy white and ivory. ◆ "It's much more comfortable now," said Van Runkle, whose Burmese cat, Hazel, snoozes in snug corners. "One of the many beauties of white rooms is that they make a great showcase for armfuls of prismatic flowers. New paintings, a painted chair, or vintage ivory textiles all fit in. Or I can keep the house rather strict, with no frou-frou. That feels so cool and peaceful on torrid summer days." ◆ White is calm, always unruffled. ◆ "My inspiration for these white rooms originally came from a passage in Isak Dinesen," said the designer. "She described the blue air in a house at certain hours. It happens here. Sometimes on autumn nights, when the French doors

Artist/designer Van Runkle's beamed living room is composed for comfort—
for her guests, for herself, and for her cats, Hazel and Charlotte.
American hooked rugs—some vintage and rare—form plum, carnelian,
nectarine, and cerulean islands on the pristine white floor. The sofa slipcover,
Van Runkle's own stitchery, is in linen from Diamond Foam & Fabric.

In summer, the house, all air and light, has a transparent, vaporous quality. Canyon light filters into the house through two tall windows and four sets of French doors. Winters, the furniture seems to gather around the fireplace. The designer is also a gifted stylist, effortlessly arranging rare books, mercury glass candlesticks, quirky lamps, shells, flowers, paintings, and linens in captivating tabletop tableaux.

are open, the maritime fog floats into the house. The air seems white, ghostly. I light the lights. They glow eerily. It's all very ethereal." ♦ Still, she didn't want the rooms to be affected or mannered—or too icy white. ♦ Walls and the ceiling are warm white. The floor is glossy pure chalky white. Van Runkle covered dining chairs in a subtle white and taupe striped linen. Her camelback sofa, all curves, is striped in pale taupe and white with black pinstripes. ♦ "White is a great color to work with because there are so many whites—and they all go together wonderfully," said Van Runkle. For embroidered silks, paint, lamps, tabletops, candlesticks, and pillows, she used white in tones of eggshell, ecru, ivory, and shell, Navaho white, and a vintage white that looks tea-dipped. ♦ Theadora Van Runkle is a fearless remodeler. ♦ In the most recent renovation of her house, Van Runkle decided to raise the roof of her living room to give it more light and air. She had skylights and roof beams added, installed small windows where there were once just attic vents, and wrapped the house with a wide verandah. ♦ Still, the house does not have the "added-on" or "recently remodeled" quality that afflicts so many formerly charming, modest houses. Guests imagine that the house has always had the same lofty ceilings, French doors, and sunny outlook. ♦ "When you're renovating a small cottage, it's important to keep every change and addition in the spirit of the original," said Van Runkle. "If possible, it's wise to choose similar traditional materials, crafted in the same manner. I did not try to impose hefty new doors or hard-edged lighting on this house. And I was always vigilant as craftsmen worked on floors and new doorways to be sure that everything was done with a light touch. The effect must be seamless, effortless."

Van Runkle, a dab hand with a paintbrush, quickly transformed an old green wicker chair into this white-painted oasis of calm. As Swedish chatelaines often do, she places her dining chairs along the wall. It's a sensible and harmonious arrangement.

"In winter I like to write in my journal or draw or paint the cats, so I appreciate comfortable chairs and corners with good light," Van Runkle said. It's very quiet in the living room in the late afternoon, and beautiful warm light shines through the trees.

"Some afternoons in the summer, the white light makes my house feel as if I'm living in a Matisse fishbowl," said Van Runkle. "The marvelous thing about white rooms is that there's no color or pattern to distract you, so you become very aware of the way sunlight comes in, and how the light changes from season to season. You also see the shapes of furniture more clearly. White shows everything off well."

One of the most coveted insider invitations is to her Sunday sketch club. In winter, watercolorists gather to paint passionately for the day. The round tabletop becomes a stage for tall candlesticks, books, and flowers, rather like a painting—or a dinner party waiting to happen. Van Runkle's crystal and pressed glass glow in the afternoon sunlight. Draperies are white Belgian linen.

Attorney Andy Gillin and his wife, Sharon, a psychologist-turned-antiques-dealer, love happy colors. That's evident on every wall of

their East Bay Hills Victorian, where colors fairly vibrate and put the rooms in a sunny mood all year. ♦ Their interior designer,

Stephen Shubel, had the walls painted buttery yellow. Moldings were painted sharp white for emphasis. ♦ So in tune are client and decorator

that they're like longtime friends who have gone the rounds of decorating for many years. In fact, Shubel and Sharon Gillin

met only last year, introduced by their hairdresser, Jane Camp, who thought they would get along famously. They do. ♦ "I loved the house

as soon as I saw it," said Shubel. "It was built in the 1880s, one of the first in the East Bay Hills, but it's not Victorian-cutesy.

The floor plan is gracious, the rooms are well-proportioned. It has great bones." ♦ The decorator pushed his clients to paint the white

walls stronger colors to give the interiors pizzazz. ♦ "When you have good, high ceilings—these are 14 feet—you can use strong colors and

not feel closed in," he said. ♦ The Gillins also liked his idea of making a perfectly cohesive background with good floor coverings and

draperies—and then funking it up. ♦ "It's hard to find clients who don't take decorating too seriously," said Shubel. "The Gillins

considered every aspect of design with care, but they also understood the importance of having fun with it."

The Gillins' Shabby Chic down-filled sofa is covered with
washable white cotton damask. The vintage coffee table with its fanciful,
curvy legs, seems about to dance a jig. Its new top is travertine.
The table's from Maison d'Etre, an eccentric style store in Oakland.
The verdigris-painted chair, its cane charmingly the worse for
wear, adds an insouciant air to the room. It's a beloved family heirloom.

The Gillins liked the concept of keeping the interiors quite simple, with the enrichment of a few special things. ♦ "It's like the idea of wearing a simple white cotton T-shirt with a great Armani jacket," said Sharon. "Everything doesn't have to be precious." ♦ Shubel is a pro in the art of mismatching. He also did a brilliant job of placing accessories and furniture. ♦ "Steve kept everything focused," the Gillins agreed. "He could see the gestalt—the big picture—and edit out anything that didn't contribute to a balanced design." ♦ Down-filled pillows on the living room sofa are a casual mix of faded old chintz, English ticking stripes, and washed linen damask. ♦ Behind the painted bench beside the sofa spirals a French handmade bent wire lamp crowned with a jaunty Kraft paper chapeau shade. A skinny copper-mesh-shaded lamp stands in narrow contrast to the overstuffed chairs and sofa. ♦ "We put comfort and function first, planning lots of places to sit in," said Sharon Gillin. ♦ On the waxed hardwood floors, the decorator used unfussy sisal carpets bound in natural linen tape. ♦ Gillin is particularly pleased that many of the accessories were purchased from the shops of friends. The French dish towels that now grace the dining chairs were purchased from the San Francisco store of Sue Fisher King, Sharon's sorority sister. The French clock above the mantel is from Blake's in Los Angeles.

The merry mix-and-match French dining chairs from Legend Antiques are striped in raspberry and cream cotton chintz from the Nya Nordiska collection at Randolph & Hein. For the family's amusement, some chair backs are covered in French dish towels with a culinary theme. Others are in chintz with narrow stripes. Draperies in white cotton denim were made by Susan Chastain. Above the French dresser, the stained-glass window is original to the house. The pique-assiette fireplace surround was made with Limoges gold-rimmed family heirloom plates broken accidentally during the remodel. Above the mantel: a gilded French mirror, a find at Tail of the Yak in Elmwood.

Easy does it: A Ginsberg Collection wicker chair adds comfort to the sitting room adjacent to the kitchen. The chair and sofa are covered in relaxed washed cotton denim by Henry Calvin Fabrics, a favorite of Stephen Shubel. The old French clock was found in a Los Angeles antique shop.

The Provencal dining table is from Sue Fisher King. French chairs, of uncertain parentage, are pillowed in white denim with bronze denim piping. The tinted cement fireplace surround and countertops were crafted by Philip Baird. The fireplace mantel was painted by Dominique Harrington of Sun Valley. When the Gillins bought their house, the remodeled kitchen, opposite, had a bland, cookie-cutter look. "It just didn't feel soulful," said Sharon Gillin.

Odom and Kate Stamps live in the pleasant Park La Brea neighborhood of Los Angeles—but truly they inhabit a world of their own creation. ♦ The style references in their poetic house come not from California but are inspired by English country houses, Belgravia townhouses, Louisiana country houses, New Orleans mansions, and recherche corners of the Northeast. ♦ "I wanted the look of our place to be indefinable—a sort of 'Lord Hoot 'n' Shoot in Malta,' " joked Odom, an architect and landscape designer. "I wanted the influences to be from everywhere and nowhere in particular. We toss together all our favorite things—with some of John Fowler's relaxed approach to style." ♦ He is referring to the great English interiors historian and decorator, a partner of Sibyl Colefax, whose own rooms showed a great love of noble-but-quirky antiques, luscious fabrics, and an appreciation of humble elegance. Fowler's grand rooms were never pompous, and his cottages never twee. ♦ "We decorate for ourselves with layer on layer on layer of collections that have caught our eye," said Kate Stamps, an in-demand interior designer. "Our decor is object-generated. We especially like harmonious, slightly faded-looking colors, and paintings, old fabrics, lamps, and furniture that have an interesting history." ♦ The couple, who lived in New Orleans when they were first married, moved to Los Angeles eight years ago. ♦ "Everything we live with here has meaning and memories for us," said Kate.

Friends love to dally in Kate and Odom's sitting room, riffling through books and decorating magazines and nestling in the cushy chairs and sofa. Natural herringbone linen covers the sofa. It is piled with pillows made of fragments of tapestry and French gold-thread embroidered textiles. The "Robin" chair, left, is covered with Colefax & Fowler "Old Rose" chintz. "Old Rose" also covers their bergere. The French window seat, center, is covered with "Seaweed" by Colefax & Fowler. The Stamps's collection of drawings, oils, and watercolors includes an oil on paper by Ludmilla von Trapp.

Kate and Odom's conviction—in the land of flea markets and swap meets—is that it is always wisest to buy the best antiques and paintings they can afford. They plan to live with their treasures forever. ♦ "We don't buy things that necessarily make sense at the time," said Kate. "Both of our mothers had antiques stores, and we gained an understanding of quality, and of rarity. We're never thinking about 'what goes with what.' Interesting things you love always look wonderful together." ♦ The dining room is small in size and full of charm. The Stampses have mastered the art of presto-chango and can turn it from a day-to-day office to a glamorous dining room in minutes. ♦ The mutable Tuscan pink tone of the walls feels cheerful during the day, when the sun pours golden light through tussah silk draperies. By candlelight, the wall color seems deeper and richer, and the stippled texture takes on a palazzo mood. The versatile dining chairs are country Hepplewhite, circa 1800. ♦ Kate and Odom have a passion for gardens, too. Through French doors, the family can step out into a shaded garden, which in turn opens to a private lawn. ♦ Around the shady pergola grow euphorbia, abutilon, geraniums, salvia, hydrangeas, and a rampant passion vine. 'Iceberg' and 'Lordly Oberon' roses do particularly well there. It's a happy habitat, too, for their cockatoo, Sinbad. ♦ Perhaps not surprising for residents of Los Angeles, the Stampses are extremely knowledgeable about film and have an enviable video collection. The collection is carefully stored in an antique bookshelf in their bedroom. The television is kept on the upper shelves of an antique French oak linen press in their bedroom. ♦ Even their daughter, Emma, sleeps in great style. The English and French fabrics in her bedroom are sweet and flowery but never sentimental. Her bed is draped with a vintage Colefax & Fowler voile. Odom stenciled her walls in romantic flowers. ♦ Emma's antique furniture has such character, you might expect it to dance around at night. A Boston cottage chest, a Regency wing chair upholstered in block chintz, and a Regency fainting couch all have great presence.

In Kate and Odom Stamps's dining room, a Picasso illustration from Lysistrata stands on a serpentine Hepplewhite chest. Odom gave the walls their poetic Tuscan pink hue, using a traditional dry-brush technique. The draperies in hand-woven tussah silk were formerly in the library of their New Orleans house.

Perchance to dream: The turn-of-the-century stately mahogany bed was Odom's grandparents' bed.

They lived in Hammond, Louisiana. The portrait is eighteenth-century Swedish. Fabrics are by Lee Jofa.

The walls were given a strie effect with a North-Atlantic-in-a-storm blue/green/gray glaze.

Antique French silk with silver and gold threads was used to drape the window.

DR. DAN SIEDLER'S COTTAGE ON RUSSIAN HILL

Radiologist Dan Siedler bought a tumbledown Craftsman cottage on Russian Hill six years ago and turned it into his

dream house. ♦ The handsome four-story house, overlooking San Francisco Bay and Treasure Island, was built in 1923 by a ship's captain.

Over the years the house had been remodeled with poor-quality materials and with little respect for the original sensibility

and architecture. It had also been stripped and divided into two apartments. Still, because of its intact timbered exterior, the city had

deemed it "architecturally significant." ♦ When Siedler bought it in 1990, little remained of the original Craftsman cottage but

the appealing facade and one paneled room. After he moved in he was shocked to discover that the roof leaked in the first winter rain.

There was no heat. He had to light the old tiled fireplace to keep warm. ♦ "I thought this cottage would be a simple remodel, a fast fix-up,"

recalled Siedler. "In the end I gave two years of my life to see it through." ♦ Siedler was fortunate to meet architectural designer

Daren Joy of North American Stijl Life (NASL) at a housewarming party. He told Joy he wanted the house to be warm, gracious, and open,

but with a mysterious quality to it. ♦ "I dreamed of a house that was rather spare that was going to inspire me to live not

only a comfortable life, but a decent one," he mused.

Dan Siedler originally bought the house because he loved the quiet

neighborhood, but the 1923 facade, with its balconies, enclosed tiled porch,

and massive timbers, soon won him over. He found the tall old cabinet

at a parochial school salvage sale. In the glass-fronted top cupboards he displays

Russel Wright dinnerware in pleasantly "dated" and dissonant colors

like pale lemon, taupe/gray, pale lavender, and tan. Stacked plates have a

rather abstract, sculptural quality.

Siedler and Joy's new interiors stand out because of
the integrity of their renovation. They did a lot of the work
themselves. The interiors have a great sense of restraint
and style. Materials, finishes, trims, and hardware are all
beautifully edited, and the mix of materials is very innovative.
With copper wall panels and minimalist stair rails as a
unifying element, the stair landing, second-floor stairway, and
dining room walls become a thrilling event.

Soon after Siedler moved in, reality set in. ♦ During a rare cold snap, all the pipes outside the building froze and burst. Sprays of water created ice sculptures in the garden. ♦ "It was like living in an abandoned building," he recalled. "I lived in one room, ate most of my meals at the hospital, and wondered if I had made a terrible mistake." ♦ It was Joy's idea to phase the project by rebuilding the shell first. As it turned out, this meant plywood floors and no kitchen for two years. ♦ Joy planned a modern version of a Craftsman cottage, rejecting the notion of a pure but boring restoration. ♦ "Because of its historical status, the city was tough on any changes to the house," Siedler said. "Getting permits to proceed was a very arduous process. It was a slow start." ♦ They fashioned a new center for the house around an open kitchen. They filled the rooms with light from new skylights, and added new French doors on the back of the top three floors. ♦ One stroke of brilliance was to incorporate whimsical found materials with sleek industrial steel, cast concrete, and aluminum-colored stained wood. ♦ Joy and Siedler reveled in the house's time-warp design. For the living-room they found a venerable redwood cabinet salvaged from a Catholic girls' school. A glossy sheer green stain gives the old woodwork new life.

Romantic vintage bronze lamps with stained-glass shades contrast with rolled-steel stair rails. ♦ In the dining room, one of the few intact parts of the house, Eames and Thonet chairs from the fifties co-exist happily with the original twenties redwood paneling. ♦ Joy fixed old Craftsman lamps in the dining room and foyer. Siedler got in the spirit by staining and Varathaning the kitchen cabinets. ♦ They chose beechwood floors, redwood moldings stained red and green, and birch plywood cabinets for several rooms. ♦ "Along the way, I learned so much about architecture and the importance of natural light, the grace of simple spaces," said Siedler. "Every surface has a richness I never envisioned." ♦ When his house was completed, Siedler was so happy with the structure, its very tactile and individual detailing, and the play of light on copper walls that he decided to keep furniture to a minimum. ♦ "Dan didn't want to clutter the house," said Joy. "He was into shedding old furniture and just having a sofa, chairs, and dining table that he feels a true connection with." ♦ "I collect art, but suddenly it feels rather redundant," added Siedler. "The richness is in the beautiful rough-hewn timber beams, the light spilling in through skylights, and surprises like the pivoting windows in the bathroom. Daren has great ideas, freely imagined." ♦ Siedler views the great changes — to his house and in his life — with deep appreciation. ♦ "Ten years ago, I didn't have time to think of aesthetic things," he said. "This has been a wonderful opportunity to express myself. I wouldn't say it was easy, but it has been more than worthwhile."

The only room in the house that did not need to be changed was the dining room, with its redwood paneling and timbered balcony overlooking flowering plum trees and a quiet Russian Hill street. The sensibility of the fifties Eames and Thonet chairs and table lives comfortably with the original Arts & Crafts timbering and light fixtures. The room is particularly romantic in the late afternoon, when western light flickers through the purple leaves of the plum trees.

ELIZABETH IVES MANWARING & TIM PERKS'S COTTAGE IN SAN FRANCISCO

San Francisco graphic designer Elizabeth Ives Manwaring is admired by her friends for her knack for finding great, affordable city dwellings. In 1992, she and her husband, architect Tim Perks, were searching through newspaper ads for a new city house. ♦ "Everything we saw was too expensive or horrible," recalled Elizabeth, who remained optimistic. ♦ "One ad caught my eye: Russian Hill Cottage, Rose Garden with Balcony," she said. ♦ As she and Perks walked down the passageway to the house, the scent of roses came to greet her. ♦ "I knew that instant that we would live there," Manwaring said. ♦ What they found in a rose garden behind a row of Victorian flats was a tiny, two-story earthquake cottage, built as quick shelter just after the 1906 earthquake and fire. It had a little Juliet balcony with delicately scrolled wrought-iron railings. But the charm almost stopped there. ♦ "The interior was terrible, but I knew that the house could be wonderful," said Manwaring. ♦ Upstairs was a bedroom, living room, an eat-in kitchen and three miniscule closets adding up to six hundred square feet. Downstairs, measuring a neat three hundred square feet, were two offices. ♦ They moved in a week later and began taking down fifties light fixtures and dirty, moth-holed draperies. They painted all the walls, scoured the floors. ♦ "We chose simple garden-y colors like celadon, wheat, ivory, pale buttercup—with lots of white trim to make it a very indoor/outdoor place," said Manwaring.

The tiny, sunny living room overlooks the rose garden. French doors, left, open to a tiny balcony. Poetic, pale celadon sets a dreamy mood. The coffee table is an old Mexican village-crafted piece from The Gardener. In contrast, the couple enjoy their Italian gold-leafed chair, circa 1950, discovered in a Polk Street antiques store. Manwaring and Perks use an old English pine armoire to store clothing and shoes. (One of the few drawbacks of the cottage is that it offers little storage.)

On the painted dresser are framed photographs,
flowers, French postcards, necklaces, and a Japanese sewing
box. The 1920 silver mirror was a wedding gift.

A gilded, monogrammed sunburst, a wedding gift, hangs
like a particularly lucky talisman above the bed. Manwaring
uses her collection of vintage quilts and French linens
every day. The antique headboard is from Shabby Chic.

Manwaring and Perks's kitchen is a gallery for Mexican retablos from Morelia, along with Roman etchings and Italian pottery. The Parisian garden chairs are from Smith & Hawken. Classic and comfortable, the antique French garden table was unearthed in an obscure San Francisco antiques store.

Manwaring and Perks decided not to go the route of small-scale furniture. ♦ "The large coffee table, velvet ottomans, and armoire are generous and make the living room feel much bigger, " observed Manwaring. "It's a very cozy room, perfect for conversation." ♦ The draperies are sheer white cotton gauze. A Persian carpet in blue, red, and brown patterns the hardwood floor. Manwaring loves flowers, so floral motifs, flower drawings, old chintz, and flower paintings color the rooms. ♦ "The kitchen is really the saving grace here," said the designer. "It has jalousie windows, a large tile counter, and yellow and celadon tile wainscot, so it's practical and the colors are graphically pleasing." ♦ The kitchen is also remarkably expansive. ♦ "We entertain a lot and are always amazed how many people can fit here," said Manwaring. "We've had parties of 40 people and served an elegant dinner." ♦ The allure of the interior can only go so far, however. ♦ "We'd stay here for ever—even though this cottage really is too small for us, parking in the neighborhood is terrible, the cottage is musty in the autumn, and it's cold in the winter," averred Manwaring. ♦ No doubt she will use her known talent to find the next perfect house.

ELEANOR & NORMAN MOSCOW'S HOUSE IN THE CLAREMONT

Eleanor Moscow has a deep and loving appreciation of her house. And indeed, its evocative design, roller-coaster history, and riparian

setting seem to imbue it with magic and mystery. It stands on a hillside above Berkeley surrounded by romantic sycamores, park-like

private gardens, and landmark Arts & Crafts houses and studios by Julia Morgan, Ernest Coxhead, and Willis Polk. Hers is a neighborhood that

harbors Nobel laureates, poet laureates, and intellectuals. One imagines behind every hedge a genius at work. ♦ Life is calm and

rather understated in this Arcadian setting. ♦ Eleanor and Norman Moscow discovered their house 22 years ago. Built in 1923 for the dean

of mining and engineering at the University of California at Berkeley, it's in an area of the Berkeley Hills originally designed by Frederick

Law Olmstead to be a natural setting on the edges of the city. Along the green edges of their lower garden, a natural creek splashes

year-round. ♦ "Neighborhood lore has it that the house was designed by the architects Reed & Corlett to be a replica of a hunting lodge in the

wilds of Scotland," mused Eleanor Moscow, an admired interior designer and antiques dealer. Her husband is a radiologist. ♦ Over the years,

the history of Berkeley invaded the house ever more insistently. In the sixties, the property became the headquarters of a lively

commune. Members kept cows, chickens, and ducks in the garden but somehow had the good sense not to change the architecture of the

In the verdant landscape of the Moscows' garden, lavender, azaleas, rhododendrons, and

buckeyes grow particularly well—assuring a colorful and fragrant surrounding for their house.

Eleanor Moscow's approach is eclectic, not didactic. She has no intention of recreating a

Maine cottage or a Scottish lodge. Theme decorating is not to her taste. Plain white walls—

no cliché stencils or faux plaster here—form a perfect, modest canvas for her very sculptural

furniture. The muted tones of her furniture and hooked rugs from New England,

France, Cornwall, and Wales seem to have been dyed by ancient herbs and wild cottage

flowers. The ottoman is upholstered in simple khaki and white French twill ticking. On the

mantel, sit a French art populaire *pine-cone cachepot and an English tole tray.*

house or pilfer from its charming interiors. ◆ Eleanor Moscow has followed her own muse in decorating her rooms. Avoiding the heavy-handed Arts & Crafts style that many in Berkeley succumb to, she has instead fashioned lighthearted, fresh-looking interiors that recall summers on the coast of Maine. ◆ "I like a very pared-down feeling," mused Moscow. "There's a certain museum-spare look, but this house is very much lived in." ◆ Eleanor Moscow likes to live with her antiques—not set them on a pedestal. ◆ Appropriately, she keeps fabrics and upholstered furniture in her rooms somewhat minimal, with little pattern. ◆ "I have a particular fondness for furniture made for themselves by untutored people, working in indigenous woods such as sycamore and fruitwoods," Moscow noted. "I feel an affinity for rather primitive cottage pieces from the provinces of France, from the West of England, from remote parts of Scandinavia, and from Maine and Vermont. They're unpretentious and untainted by the influences of the big city." ◆ Eleanor Moscow always seeks out the purest examples of cottage furniture and prefers pieces that have not been restored. Chipped legs, off-kilter legs, cracked frames, faded paint, nicks in wooden bowls, and tabletops worn smooth over time are all part of their pull. ◆ Her seventeenth-century Welsh bookcase has its original painted interior. In it, she displays early eighteenth-century French and American jasperware in mottled amber, brown, green, and ivory, several of them chipped and showing pleasing signs of age. ◆ She also collects paintings, most of them celebrating the beauties of the natural world, and prefers the hand-carved original frames. ◆ Even the hooked rugs collected over thirty years of summers in Maine are in a very subtle palette. They're calm islands of color on the ribbon mahogany floors.

Appropriate design always has lasting value. Eleanor Moscow's living room is today much as she planned it twenty years ago. The plump chair upholstered in black and white cotton is an early Angelo Donghia design. Moscow purchased her down-filled sofa in England and had it upholstered in traditional khaki-and-white-cotton ticking. The hooked rugs are Early American. Nothing about these rooms is obvious, shiny-new or pretentious. The Orkney Islands rush chair beside the sofa has a Welsh paisley quilted coverlet and a cushion covered in seventeenth-century French textiles.

The Moscows have not changed the architecture of their
1923 house at all. In fact, the simple Scottish Lodge–influenced
Arts & Crafts Revival staircase leading from the entry to
the upstairs bedrooms could hardly be improved upon. Leaded
windows and the beautifully detailed doors are all
original. Waxed floors are ribbon mahogany.

A long, narrow seventeenth-century sideboard holds an
English equine portrait and a collection of Tuscan pottery bean
bowls, a Pennsylvania bowl made of patterned paper,
and an Early Scandinavian bride's box. Flowers are by Verdure.
Above an English chest of drawers, Eleanor Moscow hangs a
Scottish pine mirror carved in a thistle pattern. The vase is
from Rhodes, the bowls from Catalonia.

Creating style is, in great measure, simply being consistent in your passions. The common thread here is refinement, subtlety, and understatement. In her ode to simplicity, Eleanor Moscow assembles pristine-white heirloom bed linens, an eighteenth-century French bed, a Scandinavian painted corner cabinet, and a French leather swivel chair in a perfectly white room. Moscow has a lively appreciation of ingenious multipurpose cottage furniture. The back of her Swedish hand-carved chair folds forward, and the chair becomes a well-balanced round table.

The quilted coverlet is Welsh, the antique quilted bedcover of white cotton is from the South of France. Everything here is carefully considered, the best of its kind, and practical as well as beautiful. Still, Eleanor Moscow wears her erudition lightly. A pair of early eighteenth-century English cottage tables set on each side of the bed are poised to hold lamps, books, flowers. Old rugs warm the floor. The intention is to make inviting, heartening rooms — not a museum.

CEVAN FORRISTT'S FARMHOUSE IN SAN JOSE

Landscape designer Cevan Forristt is an intrepid traveler. Years before Vietnam, Burma, and Cambodia were considered wise destinations—let alone fashionable—he set off from California to immerse himself in their day-to-day life, music, arts and crafts, and religious traditions. ♦ "I especially appreciated houses and temples that have stood for centuries surrounded by turmoil," recalled Forristt, whose imaginative garden plans are popular with young Silicon Valley tycoons. "I love old village arts and crafts. To me they represent, in the best way, the continuity of life, and an altruistic belief in the power of creativity and the human spirit." ♦ Forristt returned from his trips with antique painted architectural fragments, lacquerware, carved Cambodian chairs, Buddha sculptures, hand-carved wooden offering bowls, and a lifetime's supply of village textiles. ♦ Six years ago, Forristt discovered a 120-year-old farm cottage on a sheltered quarter-acre of land in a quiet neighborhood not far from downtown San Jose. ♦ "The house had been completely neglected and was just an empty shell," said Forristt. "It was also pretty small—just 910 square feet. What I was really drawn to was the land, with two great old persimmon trees." ♦ Forristt bought the property knowing that he could perform magic and transform the garden. ♦ "My friends told me to bulldoze the house, but I could already visualize the high ceilings, the well-shaped rooms, the peace and privacy," he recalled. "The blessing was that the house had no termites." ♦ Forristt then set off on another journey—the careful renovation of his farm cottage. ♦ He cleared

The interiors of the formerly derelict farmhouse glow with colors of Forristt's Asian textiles. On his carved and gilded teak Thai bed, purchased in Bangkok, he piles a vivid array of Thai pillows. In the foreground is a Burmese offering vessel. Green and gold Balinese textiles (bought for a song at a small town near Denpasar) also completely disguise the room's humble origins.

the land and planted tangerine and orange trees, eight varieties of Asian pears, a vegetable garden, and a high bamboo hedge. He jacked the house up eight feet and built a solid foundation and a new basement. ♦ "I've used everything from my travels in my house," said the gardener. It now looks more like the Java Sea than San Jose. ♦ In the dining room Forristt displays a gold-leafed Thai Buddha on top of a Vietnamese cabinet. Burmese lacquerware and offering bowls are arranged like sculpture around the living room. He painted walls of the hallway an ancient-looking olive green, trimmed kitchen cabinets and doors with vivid orange, and one morning during breakfast felt inspired to paint the interior of a cabinet egg-yolk yellow. ♦ "I'm a true collector, so I'll go traveling again soon to find more artifacts for my house and my garden," said Forristt. "Each day my house and my collections take me away from everyday cares into another world. And every moment I feel so lucky."

In his dining room—Cevan Forristt is an adventurous cook—the designer sets out colorful collections of Asian handcrafts. Forristt made the massive hand-hewn mortise-and-tenon redwood table from recycled timber. Old windows are original to the farmhouse. The Far East mood is enhanced with architectural fragments and old Chinese window screens. Earthy wall paints were mottled to look ancient. The landscape designer opens his kitchen window to the garden, and gives the utilitarian room an almost tropical feeling.

It's a garden, not an architectural dig: Marble columns and carved granite architectural fragments in his private back garden were discovered at a Central California stonemason's.

Cevan Forristt's garden is a folly, a fantasy. He began with an empty, unfenced back lot measuring seventy-five feet by eighty feet. A new high stucco wall topped with old terra-cotta tiles (to simulate a roof overhang) formed a private courtyard. ♦ He planted Japanese timber bamboo and Bamboo "Robert Young." "Bamboo gives a lush, verdant look year-round," said Forristt. "At two o'clock every afternoon in the summer, the wind rises and the rustling sound is very mysterious." ♦ Forristt has let the bamboo proliferate so that the garden seems unplanned and wild. Two or three times a year he trims it back and thins its culms so that the growth is not too dense. ♦ "It seems as if it happened by chance and is undesigned, but it's very controlled," said Forristt of his muscular bamboo, broken columns of granite, ancient Mexican grinding stones, old Spanish stone sinks, reflecting ponds, and Japanese foo dogs. ♦ "The stone represents ancient Western chivalry and manners, and the bamboo symbolizes the Pacific and new tendrils of the East enhancing the ancient culture," Forristt noted. ♦ The climate in San Jose is mild all year, so Forristt often cooks salt-baked prawns and other delicacies outdoors. ♦ Some bamboo culms have now reached as high as sixty feet. "Birds rest there at night. In the summer a mockingbird often visits," Forristt said. "I can hear it practicing tunes up in the leaves. Its a capella music sounds like jazz improvisation."

Alice Erb is extremely fortunate to have a bossy younger sister. ♦ Twelve years ago, Susan, her beloved sis, admired a compound of

four old houses on a quiet block-long street in Oakland. She found out the estate was for sale. It had charmingly overgrown gardens,

three old wells, a giant walnut tree, and healthy old fig, plum, lemon, lime, and pomegranate trees. Erb's sibling insisted that Alice and three

friends band together and purchase the property. ♦ Felicitously, Erb, who is a co-owner, with Lauren Allard, of the 25-year-old Elmwood shop,

Tail of the Yak, also loved the houses and she and architect Tom Dolan and Ernie McClintock put in their bid. ♦ "I was hiking in the

Canyon de Chelly in Arizona, and via a pay phone at the rim I heard that our offer had been accepted," Erb recalled, still rather amazed. ♦

The compound had originally been built by an Italian family that had owned the land for 100 years. When the grandmother died in

1980, the family put it up for sale. ♦ "Fortunately, the house I selected was in good order, because the others two were in disarray," said Erb,

who was not prepared for major remodeling. ♦ Her "re-do" merely involved a few years of carefully undoing insensitive renovations

from the fifties. Erb pulled up old carpets and linoleum, and removed fake redwood paneling. The house now looks as if it had slept through

the last 70 years undisturbed . . . to be awakened by Alice Erb with her magic touch.

Alice Erb has the best of both worlds: a stand-alone bungalow, privacy
in proximity to two dear friends, and a hidden garden next door that bursts
forth each spring with climbing roses and old-fashioned perennials.
In the garden, which Erb co-owns with her chums, sky-high 'Cecile Brunner'
and 'Iceberg' roses run rampant over hedges and attract bees and butterflies.
David Austin roses scent the air in the sunny, dry East Bay climate. Along the
garden path, irises, 'Sally Holmes' roses and several kinds of lavender add
dashes of lively color. Flowers from the garden grace her white bedroom.

In her living room, which glows in the afternoon sunlight, Alice Erb painted walls a luscious celadon. The chimneypiece was painted a warm terra-cotta to give it definition and architectural distinction. Arts & Crafts tiles are original to the house. The Big Ben clock is a particularly fine piece of hobo art, discovered at the Ames Gallery in Berkeley.

Serendipity plays a role in Erb's rooms. The old wool/mohair sofa was a gift from a friend. On the mantel, Erb's collections include cast lead figures, Mexican retablos, French candelabras, and mirrored fruit. Birds' nests were gifts from her friend Carrie Glenn.

Erb discovered that the back of her house had been built in 1890, and the front, in the style of a California bungalow, was added in the twenties after a fire. ♦ "I had to put on a new roof, but you would expect that," said the mild-mannered Erb, who recently painted the exterior pale cream. ♦ Erb's style is engagingly eccentric. Rooms and colors break all sorts of rules of decoration and seem all the better for going their own way. ♦ "I like living with beautiful things in a spare manner," Erb observed. "I can't live with too much visual distraction." ♦ It is also her nature to surround herself with old rugs from Turkey and Iran, folk art from Mexico, textiles from North Africa, and American tramp and hobo art. In the early seventies, she started traveling throughout the Middle East to buy jewelry, paintings, folk crafts, and rich silk quilts and rugs for the original owners of Tail of the Yak. (The shop was originally named by a Tibetan lama, who said the stalwart beast's tail was considered a sign of good luck in the Himalayas.) ♦ "I have a sense of euphoria when I bring old ikats and handwoven textiles back from Africa or Turkey or Morocco," said Erb, who still travels into the heart of Mexico to find village pottery and festive fabrics, and to the South of England to find antique jewelry. ♦ Poetic hues are her particular talent. Her bedroom has walls of pale periwinkle. The kitchen decor mixes ancient rose tones and pale matte green the color of calla lily stems. Walls in the living room are celadon, with a dash of blue. ♦ "I see that wall color as winter dawn chartreuse," said Erb. "I wanted it to be a color you couldn't quite describe, so that it would look different throughout the day, throughout the year." ♦ To give the effect of a wainscot, Erb painted a scallop and rose motif around the wall.

Alice Erb's study was originally the dining room. The pine table and armoire were left in the house by the previous owner. Erb covers the table with Tunisian textiles. Here, she surrounds herself with old books and joyful Mexican crepe paper marigolds in a Oaxacan black pottery vase. She keeps an upright piano in one corner but admits, with regret, that she seldom has time to play. The chair, possibly nineteenth-century Italian, was a discovery in the back room of Jack's Antiques, a Berkeley institution. The rug is Tunisian.

Erb's kitchen takes a cosmopolitan spin. Her dining table is a New England pine farm table. The white-painted urn vase was a $2 "junko" find from one her favorite sources, Jack's Antiques, in Berkeley. In the wall cabinets, original to the house, she keeps Dedham ironstone plates, old enameled tureens, and Portuguese and Mexican hand-painted ceramics.

Two ceramic plates by the Oaxacan Aguilar sisters—considered Mexican living treasures—hang on the luscious green wall above the white-painted wainscot.

I N CALIFORNIA, INTERIOR DESIGN AND ARCHITECTURE BOW TO NATURE. ◆ COUNTRY ARCHITECTURE AND

INTERIOR DECORATION DON'T EVEN TRY TO COMPETE WITH THE CRAGGY COAST, HILLS SCULPTED BY THE WIND AND RAIN,

THE ETERNAL REDWOODS, THE SNOW-CROWNED SIERRA, OR RUST-RED AUTUMN VINES IN THE NAPA

VALLEY. ◆ THE BEAUTY CONTEST HAS BEEN WON, SO THE BEST ARCHITECTS AND DESIGNERS CRAFT HOUSES THAT ARE

SUBTLE, SITE-FRIENDLY, UNPRETENTIOUS, APPROPRIATE, AND NEVER SLICK. IT'S POINTLESS TO LORD IT OVER

THE LANDSCAPE. ◆ UNLIKE OTHER PARTS OF THE COUNTRY—NOTABLY MAINE, CONNECTICUT, NEW MEXICO—CALIFORNIA

COUNTRY HAS NO ONE VERNACULAR ARCHITECTURE. OLD WOODEN FARMHOUSES, SIMPLE AND HONEST, HAVE A

NATURAL, HARMONIOUS FEELING. BUT SO DO WONKY VICTORIANS, SHINGLED SHACKS, MEDITERRANEAN-STYLE VILLAS,

AND FOREST-SHADED ARTS & CRAFTS LOG CABINS. ◆ THE SUNNY, FRENCH-DOORED PAVILION THAT NICK MEIN

AND JEFF DONEY FURNISHED IN WOODSIDE SEEMS LIKE THE COUNTRY HEADQUARTERS OF AN EXPLORER OR THE CABINET

OF CURIOSITIES OF A WORLDLY BOTANIST. THEIR NATURALISTS' STUDY WAS ONCE A HAYLOFT DOWN-TO-EARTH

ROMANTICS, THEY ALSO DID AN ABOUT-FACE WITH THE STABLE, TURNING THE EQUINE DOMAIN INTO RATHER *RECHERCHE*

LIVING QUARTERS. ◆ FASHION DESIGNER ISDA FUNARI SAYS HER HOUSE WAS "ONE STEP AWAY FROM A TENT" WHEN

SHE FIRST SAW IT. RATHER THAN WAIT FOR THE NEXT EARTHQUAKE TO KNOCK IT OVER, SHE AND HER PARTNER GRABBED

HAMMERS AND NAILS AND STARTED WORKING. ◆ ORLANDO DIAZ-AZCUY DOESN'T BELIEVE YOU HAVE TO LEAVE

POLISHED STYLE IN THE CITY. ON THURSDAY HE LEAVES HIS CHIC MEDITERRANEAN HOUSE IN ST. FRANCIS WOOD TO WORK

ON FURNITURE AND FABRIC DESIGNS AND COMMUNE WITH NATURE. HIS MORE-IS-MORE THEORY OF COLOR

ENRICHES THE ROOMS OF HIS MODEST COTTAGE. ◆ THE APPROACH IS AMIABLE—THERE'S NOTHING OVERDONE HERE.

THESE ARE HOUSES WITH AN EASY SERENITY.

On the Peninsula, south of San Francisco, Nick Mein and Jeffrey Doney
dreamed up a haven for themselves, and their Rhodesian Ridgebacks.
It's a bibliophile's paradise with books galore, relaxed furniture, good light,
and a peaceful prospect of the garden.

Nick Mein, a former history teacher, and architect Jeffrey Doney live in what is surely the most stylish stable in the West. Make that a former stable. ◆ Mein, a San Franciscan who had been living in Hawaii, decided four years ago to move back to his family's 16-acre estate in Woodside. There, among stately California live oaks, he rediscovered an old four-horse stable and a nearby hay shed, both built in 1965. ◆ "Those two farm buildings were honest, well-built, and very unpretentious," recalled Mein. "Three horses lived in the stable until the day I decided to turn it into my house and refashion their hayloft into a summer pavilion." ◆ Working fast, Mein and a contractor friend cleaned up the stable and completed the bare-bones construction work in six weeks. ◆ Mein and his contractor first built a new floor in the stable with rough-hewn red pine planks that had been used to divide the horse stalls. ◆ "I loved the wood because the horses had kicked it over the years and it was rather beaten up," he said. "The floor now has a feeling of age, which I think is appropriate." ◆ He and Doney added sheetrock walls and crown moldings. ◆ "It's crown moldings that are my secret of good remodeling and making something elegant from a rather humble building," said Mein. "Crown moldings—available at any hardware store or lumber yard—finish off the rooms and your eye stops there. You can have a rather rough, barn-like ceiling, as I do here, and a molding gives it refinement. There's an interval between the ceiling and wall surfaces that enhances the wall's dimension." ◆ A new fireplace was a pastiche of marble and granite Mein found on the family property.

At one end of the living room, between two sets of French doors, Mein and Doney have built a study. Tall bookshelves, a painting of St. Louis, antiques, and an old pine library table bestow a studious air. The daybed is from the Philippines. Mein and Doney like their outdoor furniture to be rather relaxed. The old stone table, purchased at auction, required nine strong people to carry it onto the terrace. Beyond the meadow, planted with spring daffodils and wildflowers, is a well-tended vegetable garden.

Delicious contrasts: Nick Mein particularly likes to cover pillows in vintage fabrics like the ikat-weave Thai silk and shimmering sari silks he inherited from his grandmother. The sofa and chairs are upholstered in natural canvas. The chandelier was unearthed in London. Mein believes the rusted-gilt piece was originally from Normandy. The 1850 Cape Dutch stinkwood cabinet at the end of the room is an heirloom from the days when the family patriarchs were mining in South Africa. It has sterling silver mounts.

The dining table, designed by George Whittell, has a Roman base with deer feet. One pair of dining chairs is Northern Italian, the other two are chic Louis XVI reproductions, "made just the other day," joked Mein.

"Poking around in a junk pile one day I found old carved pieces of marble. I even managed to put together a mantel from two broken fragments," marveled Mein. Over the mantel he placed an Italian graffito mirror painted green with gold leaf. It's surrounded by paintings of landscapes of his family's Gilroy ranches, along with scenes of Majorca, Scotland, and Mount Vesuvius. ◆ The bachelor kitchen was carved out of the former tack room. He gave the five-foot-by-twelve-foot room a floor of terra-cotta tiles, and hangs pots and pans from the ceiling. ◆ Mein restyled the living room ceiling beams. "They were two feet apart and looked too busy," he said. "I took out half of them, and it instantly lightened up the whole room and made the ceiling height more apparent." ◆ "It's a total do-it-yourself project," laughed Mein, who had remodeled nineteen Victorian houses in San Francisco in the seventies. ◆ "For decoration, I decided to just please myself and make the rooms comfortable," Mein said. "On the floors I put old kilims that my grandfather bought in Persia. I found old chandeliers—nothing too pretentious—in London and in Paris flea markets, and shipped them home. They're all things of odd provenance and slightly mysterious design. I bought a lot of things at auction." ◆ The house is a compilation of everything Mein has collected for the last 40 years. ◆ Mein's and Doney's collections—which reflect their passion for travel and the world of nature—fill every corner of the rooms.

Paintings, Belgian ceramic vases, old books, French saint portraits, artist monographs, orchids in cachepots, Italian volcano paintings, bats, shells, butterflies, minerals, core samples from South African gold and diamond mines, and dried leaves and seeds often seem to be invading the rooms. The two passionate collectors insist that they are, in fact, very narrowly focused and collect in a very single-minded fashion. ◆ "I love anything to do with deer and grab everything I find," admitted Mein. He has five Catteau Belgian ceramic vases, each with delicate blue deer gracefully circling the curved sides. There are also deer andirons, deer heads, and deer feet on the dining table. ◆ Mein has a fine montage of volcano paintings on the living room walls. ◆ "It looks like I pick up any volcano painting, but I have only Mt. Vesuvius—not Etna!" Mein insisted. "Now I don't have room for more shells or bats, so I find bat prints or shell volumes. We've just barely got room on the walls for Jeff's South American and Balinese butterflies. We're constantly moving things around." ◆ They also rebuilt a former lathe-house into a proper greenhouse for their collections of five hundred orchids. ◆ Throughout the year they bring in flowering orchids—many of them rare and some of them quite dramatic—which are beautifully presented in vintage cachepots. ◆ Doney and Mein clearly know about collecting. And they understand the fine art of devising sumptuously simple interiors that celebrate life and nature. Together they have followed their own hearts—and redefined country style.

Rhodesian Ridgebacks guard the pavilion, a former hay-barn. The sofa is slipcovered in natural canvas, comforted with a collection of colorful silk and cotton pillows. The coffee table, originally built for the Mein family's Gilroy ranch, has a pine base and a top of stretched cowhide. Wade Hoefer's sand and oil-paint landscape hangs on the wall, giving the effect of a window with a view. Displayed on all walls are bat and shell prints, and Doney's butterflies.

On a drawing board, Doney smooths out architectural prints and stacks old books. A pair of cloisonne lamps of uncertain provenance stand behind the sofa. Among Mein and Doney's prized possessions are Egyptian artifacts, Majorcan piggybanks, bats in a glass case, Chinese jade, and dried seed pods.

To the shell of a building, Doney added old windows, sheetrock walls, crown moldings, and a terra-cotta painted floor. Bolts of odd fabrics and an unusual square kilim add pattern.

Architectural salvage companies in San Francisco and Berkeley proved to be valuable sources of architectural details for the pavilion. The French doors and new mullioned windows were scrap-yard finds. The vintage pine counter, probably from a Victorian house, gives the long wall dimension. A wasp's nest, found in Tahoe, hangs in one corner.

ISDA FUNARI & TONY MELENDREZ'S HOUSE IN THE SANTA CRUZ MOUNTAINS

Fashion designer Isda Funari doesn't exactly seem like the log cabin type. ◆ Her muse and inspiration is Chanel rather than

Thoreau. ◆ But living in a log cabin among the redwoods near Boulder Creek, a historic logging town in the Santa Cruz Mountains, affords

her the peace and solitude that fuel her creativity. ◆ "Everyone imagines that a fashion designer would like a super-slick city apartment

and a glamorous life, but not me," said Funari. Her company, ISDA & CO, designs and manufactures a popular line of chic sportswear. Her

apparel is sold throughout the United States, and at her stores in Pasadena and Walnut Creek, California. ◆ "I love the simplicity

of my house and the tranquility of this small town," she said. "This is my idea of heaven." ◆ The log cabin, restored and enlarged over the last

seven years by her longtime boyfriend, builder Tony Melendrez, makes the perfect retreat. They have created a place of simple beauty

far from city bustle. ◆ Funari drives to her office in San Francisco, 90 minutes north, a couple of days a week. When she's working in her

studio, a few steps from the house, she is still within reach by fax, phone, FedEx or UPS. ◆ The 65-year old cabin is true to its

origins, down to its log-burning stove and gleaming waxed wood floors. Funari's all-white color scheme and open plan give the interior a

fresh, modern update. There's nothing faux Americana rustic or retro-kitschy here. ◆ "I nixed color and a lot of pattern because

after spending my day working with color swatches and sketches, my eyes and imagination need a break," she said. ◆ The couple discovered

the old house by chance when visiting friends in Boulder Creek. The tumbledown log cabin, surrounded by brambles, was for sale.

Eight years ago, Isda Funari and Tony Melendrez found their log cabin in sorry
condition and have slowly and thoughtfully brought it back to life. New white-framed
windows filter light into the house and give the exterior dimension and cheer.
In the living room, two sofas are covered in a simple washable white cotton and
draped with woven wool throws and quilts from New England. Walls are white plaster.
Six new skylights fill the spacious interior with daylong sun.

Funari's refined sense of order and composition are evident throughout the house. The simple pine dining table beneath the skylights is surrounded—embraced—by the rhythmic curved backs of her Windsor-style chairs. Sunlight creates pools of intense brightness in the superbly crafted interior. Consistent with her style and all-white color palette, Funari chooses armfuls of white irises for their archetypal beauty.

"The house was very small and very dilapidated," recalled Funari. "It was a couple of steps from being a tent. There was no insulation. You could see the sky through the walls." ◆ "When we first saw the house the interior was dusty and full of cobwebs," continues Funari. "But you could see that this was a place someone had once loved and taken care of. Tony and I thought it had real possibilities." ◆ Conversations with the grandson of the original owners revealed that the cabin had been built from a kit in the thirties. ◆ "Our friends thought we were nuts, but Tony and I are romantics," Isda Funari explained. "We wanted to bring the house back to the way it had looked originally—but better." ◆ Over the years they have worked on the house in spurts. ◆ "We did all the initial rebuilding and insulating and repairing, and then got comfortable and lazy," the designer said. ◆ After an earthquake toppled their chimney and damaged a wall, they enlarged the living room, built new skylights, and added new windows overlooking the garden. ◆ Funari grows pungent armfuls of basil and herbs in a clearing in the redwoods for her favorite pesto recipes. Old roses scent the air. ◆ "Nothing teaches you patience like gardening," she said. "It's been years of trial and error before I got the flowers and vegetables right." ◆ And she says she never misses the big city.

The designer, who grew up in Los Angeles, the daughter of a Sicilian father and a Mexican Indian mother, collects art books, Indonesian paintings, and textiles, folk crafts, baskets, antique silver, and hand-carved wooden bowls and arranges them on shelves and antique pine tables. ♦ Life at the mountain house has its own natural pace. ♦ Weekends, the couple is out in the fenced garden among the raised beds, encouraging tomatoes, thyme, berries, and sorrel. ♦ Outside the house, sparrows play in a stone birdbath amid a tangle of white clematis. The tall, ancient redwoods stand like noble protectors of the house, giving its inhabitants a sense of connection to the earth and a feeling of security. ♦ Nearby, the rock-strewn San Lorenzo River offers up salmon and trout. You could float 20 miles downriver to Santa Cruz on the coast if you had the time. Friends from the city love to visit, so there's hardly a shortage of good company on weekends. ♦ The house and garden are never-ending projects. ♦ "You're very lucky if you find a house and setting that suit you," noted Funari. "After traveling to Hong Kong or Paris or New York, I come home to this beautiful place and the solitude and I'm very grateful."

The new sky-lit kitchen was carved from an old, dark kitchen and a small laundry room. New windows were added at the back. Equipment includes a commercial stove and two large butcher block worktables built by Melendrez, an expert cook. New built-in cabinets house all-white dinnerware and antique silver, collected around the world. The framed trio of vintage English cigarette cards was found on London's Portobello Road.

The house had originally been used as a summer cottage and was never intended for year-round use.

Original bedrooms were rather pokey. One handsome bedroom was carved from two small bedrooms.

The room's pine furniture and deliberately simplified textures and surfaces make repose easy.

White sheets, purchased in China, are hand-embroidered. White stoneware, sculptural and

shapely, was collected on business trips around the world. Even collections of make-up brushes and

fragrances are arranged in perfect symmetry.

Residents in a certain North Berkeley neighborhood are never surprised to glimpse what appear to be rose bushes or quince trees marching down Carrie Glenn's driveway. They know the noted flower stylist is returning to her studio with country-grown flowers and wild branches of blossoms or fruit, destined for Chez Panisse or a fortunate client. ♦ Those who have been enjoying her ravishing seasonal flowers at the restaurant for 24 years would not find it startling to hear that Carrie Glenn lives in a house almost hidden behind and beneath Japanese anemones, honeysuckle, grapevines, old roses, and clematis, in a birch coppice. Her house is very Carrie. She rejects the modern and obvious, the mass-produced. ♦ "My house is a welcome retreat from the noise of the city," admitted Glenn, who first found it in 1975. "I'm surrounded by old apple trees and other people's gardens and it's as quiet as being in the country." ♦ Glenn loved the setting so much that she took a chance on the property. She knew it would take a lot of work. ♦ "The house was built as a cabin in 1912, and was the most rudimentary shelter," admitted Glenn. "It had no foundation—it was really bad." ♦ Upstairs there were two tiny bedrooms. The kitchen was rudimentary, and the dining room a mere afterthought. ♦ "I was originally a renter, so I didn't think it was a jewel but it was off-the-street and very quiet," she said. "There was nothing that originally appealed to me especially except the setting, that gave me the feeling that I was somewhere else." ♦ She first gave the weathered exterior protective walls of redwood siding, then, built a foundation. ♦ Glenn started serious work on the interior in 1986 soon after she purchased the property.

Flower stylist Carrie Glenn's prize French velvet-upholstered sofa was an antiques store trophy—for just $150. She carried it home from Sebastapol in her car, in triumph. The versatility of soothing neutral colors holds great appeal. Shutters are painted black, and the windows are stained blue/gray. Plaster walls have a gray/green tint. Her shingled house stands in a sylvan setting, just five minutes from Chez Panisse.

*Glenn worked hard and passionately to be sure that the new
kitchen looked original to the house. She eschews modern
appliances but in a nod to reality she has a practical stove,
and hides a refrigerator behind wooden slats. The floor is slate,
buffed to a soft glow. Her granite-topped antique French
pastry table was a gift from her friends at Chez Panisse, for
24 years of glorious flowers. Glenn describes her chairs
as "a motley crew." One black lacquer chair may have come
from the Brighton Pavilion.*

"I took a crowbar one night and just started ripping
out the old sheetrock walls and the hideous paneling,"
laughed the stylist and writer. "That finally started
the improvement process." ◆ Upstairs she added
French doors with balconies and rethought the two
minuscule rooms. She now has a bedroom under the
eaves and a generous dressing room with a large closet.
◆ Glenn removed the wall and door between the
kitchen and dining room to make one generous room,
with an office in one corner. ◆ "I didn't want the
usual kitchen—but rather a softer space where I can
write, prepare food, cook without having to use modern appliances, read, and dream," she said. The refrigerator is disguised with stained-wood doors so that it
won't call attention to itself—or look completely
anachronistic in the Arts & Crafts-inspired room. ◆
"I didn't want my kitchen to say, 'This is a kitchen,'"
said Glenn. "I see no reason for me to have a
dishwasher, either. I like to wash dishes by hand. I
couldn't even stand to look at a toaster. I want to take
myself back to a time when things were a little more
primitive and simple." ◆ The handsome kitchen floor
is maple with practical polished slate inset. The fir
cabinets are stained gray. All of the countertops and
the splash-back are zinc. ◆ "I like the way zinc ages
to look like an old galvanized flower bucket," she said.

"I'm sorry now that I had the fir cabinets lacquered. They're a little shinier than I'd like." ♦ Glenn views her house as a work in progress. ♦ "I haven't really finished the house, although the structure is complete," she said. "I have a Chinese chair I need upholstered, more pillows to be covered, and I want to find kitchen chairs I love." ♦ Still, the house is the grace note in her life. ♦ "I work very long days, so I appreciate the peace in my house," Glenn said. "I don't like a busy environment. The house is not exactly minimal, but I didn't go overboard with rustic ornamentation, either." ♦ Glenn appreciates every detail, down to the cobwebs on the windows, the sensual stone and wood, and the way winter sunlight slants into her bedroom. ♦ "It's my little country house—just a few minutes from the heart of Berkeley," she said.

Carrie Glenn's bedroom under the eaves feels like some faraway forest retreat. It's tiny, but French doors and petite balconies give it an airy feeling. The balcony has a distant view of the San Francisco Bay. Glenn found her French wicker chair at an eccentric antiques dealer's store in Oakland. A Haywood twenties wicker desk and chair, in the original maize-colored paint, was purchased at an antiques collective in San Anselmo. Glenn likes to arrange scented roses such as 'Sally Holmes' in a simple glass vase on her desk.

Some of the best interior designer-client relationships begin by chance. When Jessica Parish bought her Mill Valley house five years ago, her realtor happened to suggest that she might consult Sausalito interior designer Kendall Wilkinson to get started with refurbishing. The designer's trained eye proved to be invaluable, and she has been working on the house, on and off, for more than four years. ◆ Parish's secluded shingled house had been built in 1910 as a weekend getaway for a San Francisco family. At that time wealthy San Franciscans intent on escaping summer fog took a ferry across the bay to Sausalito and then a train to the Mill Valley rail depot—almost a day's journey. (The old depot's still there. It's now a cafe and book shop.) ◆ Originally a simple, cozy two-room cottage, Parish's house had been added to over the last 50 years. A large solarium (now the dining room and sitting room) facing east, and a sunny bedroom and deck on the western end of the house have been among the house's mid-century enhancements. ◆ "My client had spent parts of her childhood with her father in a sixteenth-century farmhouse in England, and wanted me to recreate that English country house feeling with an updated, romantic mood," Wilkinson said. "Jessica wanted her house to look inviting, not like a period piece." ◆ Parish, a fifth-generation San Franciscan, owned some outstanding antiques, including furniture inherited from her father and from her grandmother, the noted interior designer, "Sister" Parish. ◆ Wilkinson first developed a color palette and a furniture plan using existing pieces—and then went shopping.

Comfort and ease: Pets are part of the family here, so sofas and chairs are elegant but relaxed. The sofa, chair, and ottoman were custom-upholstered and slipcovered. The sofa's new "dress" is in linen damask. Pear and pomegranate candlesticks were crafted by Ironies. Kendall Wilkinson designed the coffee table, which has a rose marble top and a rust-finish iron base. Interior designer David Livingston designed the column lamp.

The green-painted traveling chest was a gift to Parish from her father.

Jessica Parish's house, with windows facing old-growth redwood trees, was somewhat dark when she first moved in. ◆ Working with designer David Livingston, Wilkinson painted the walls of the living room creamy white. She used her lighter antiques there. ◆ The designers devised a standard lamp from an antique wood column, and refashioned a decrepit junk-store chandelier after removing its fussy crystals and candleholders. ◆ The former sun room, added in the fifties, was full of potential but somewhat unfocused. More than thirty feet long, with arched windows on three sides, it demanded large-scale chairs and bold decorating strokes. Wilkinson reworked it into a solarium/dining room, keeping furniture arrangements loose so that the room did not feel too "done." ◆ Wilkinson placed the large English oak gate-leg farm table and a mix of antique English chairs, which Parish inherited from her father, at one end. Here Parish entertains, sets up books, or completes paperwork. At the other end of the room, Wilkinson places an overscale sofa and an upholstered club chair and ottoman. The camelback salon sofa was upholstered in beige linen. ◆ A glass-topped, iron-base coffee table holds garden books and flowers. ◆ "All along the plan was to respect the integrity and spirit of the original little cottage," said Wilkinson. They also brought the outdoors in with floral patterns and natural colors. ◆ Perhaps best of all, the house feels fresh, airy, and open. Wild nature and the changing seasons are visible from every window.

Wilkinson and Parish decided to leave the arched windows in the solarium / dining room bare. Now, redwoods and elm trees on the property provide the "curtains." Sensible sisal rugs were chosen to cover the hardwood floor.

Jessica Parish's canine companion, Makena, an Australian shepherd-mix mutt, has the run of the house. Simple linens and cottons in muted tones cover the easygoing chairs and the sofa.

Stylist/photographer/author Helie Robertson works long hours to make her bountiful one-third-acre cottage garden in Northern California look beautiful year-round. She favors a natural look, with drifts of colorful flower beds, wildflowers blooming around old Pippin apple trees, and delicate pink 'Cecile Brunner' roses spilling over a trellis and scenting her front pathway. A grapevine twines through the wisteria that shades her porch. ♦ Formality is not Robertson's style. She likes the beds to look a little wild. Still, after a day's labor with a hoe one spring, Robertson was chagrined to hear passersby snip, "What a pretty garden. Too bad they don't take care of it." ♦ "I love to experiment with new bulbs or a butterfly-meadow seed collection. My sudden enthusiasm for bright red tulips or golden California poppies can produce some wild and wonderful color combinations. Peppermint-striped tulips and crimson Oriental poppies pop up beside delicate blue forget-me-nots and ruffled pink tree peonies. Gertrude Jekyll would turn over in her grave!" joked Robertson. ♦ Like penny-conscious English cottage gardeners, Robertson trades clippings, bulbs, and seeds with her friends and neighbors. To cover fences and garden arches and give her garden structure, she planted fragrant, vigorous roses. 'Climbing Peace,' 'Talisman,' 'Climbing Mrs. Sam McGredy,' and her favorite, 'Cecile Brunner,' are a great return for her original investment of $6 each for bareroot rose bushes. ♦ Robertson has even brought wizened old plum, peach, and apricot trees back to life and harvests flavorful fruit for jewel-colored jams and jellies. ♦ It's wonderfully evident at Helie Robertson's Marin County house that she's a passionate collector and gardener. Every shelf, table, desk, stair, window ledge, cabinet, and corner is crowned with her prized green Arts & Crafts vases and bowls. Every room is bedecked with cowboy and Indian memorabilia, handsome old tin toys, dusty sombreros, witty pot-metal figures, and displays of fine hand-tinted postcards, most of her treasures bought for a song at Northern California flea markets.

'Climbing Royal Sunset' flourishes on Robertson's old shed.
The garden is very sheltered, so tender flowers, hardy climbers,
mystery transplants, and bulbs do well.

*Robertson made a home under the stairs for her green and
turquoise Arts & Crafts pottery finds. One highlight
is 'Despondency,' an urn in pale turquoise matte glaze by Van
Briggle. The design won first prize at the 1903 Paris
Salon and is now in the Louvre collection. Robertson bought
it for $250 (a steal) at a flea market.*

*Helie Robertson, in demand as a stylist for photo shoots, likes
to arrange flowers (grown from seed) in her Arts &
Crafts vases. Like dyed-in-the-wool collectors everywhere,
she presents caches of her treasures in every room.*

A virtuoso collection of sculptural Teco, Rookwood, Van Briggle, and
Weller green pottery pitchers, urns, vases, and bowls is confidently
arranged as a monochromatic tableau along a rough-hewn redwood mantel
in the living room. ◆ Souvenir Indian tepees in time-faded hues, and toy
tin cars sans paint make a nostalgic tablescape in the center of a massive
redwood coffee table. ◆ Robertson and her beau, potter/builder Joe
Wahnsiedler, started collecting more than twenty years ago, long before
flea markets became fashionable. The Sausalito flea market, which used to
take place on a picturesque patch of open space just north of the Golden
Gate Bridge, was their favorite. Like the Paris, Rome, and New York
markets they visit when they're traveling, it offered everything for the cre-
ative collector, from fine vintage clothing and old gardening books (another of Roberston's targets) to antique tools, scratched records, kitchen
gadgets, and fifties furniture. ◆ "I began buying American Arts & Crafts
pottery because I love the simple, rather austere shapes. And green is my
favorite color," said Robertson. Over the years she and Wahnsiedler have
become very discerning. They have bought reference books and museum
catalogs documenting American pottery. They've memorized the distinc-
tive logos stamped on the bottom of pottery and know when a piece is
rare, old, a steal, or overpriced. ◆ "We're also attracted to the natural
brown and beige tones of Indian weaving." she said. "We never mind signs
of wear and tear. On our Southwestern pieces, we prefer the patina of
age, a layer of dust, and nicks and chips from use. We like authentic
pieces, but we have a sense of humor about goofy souvenir stuff. You
shouldn't get too serious. ◆ "You may have been poking through piles of
junk for two hours, and be just about ready to go home for breakfast,
and suddenly you see a green Van Briggle vase with raised flower motifs.
You know it's worth more than $600, and the tired fellow running
the stall is asking $100. You hand over the cash. You carry off the vase in
triumph," said Robertson. "In a second, all those misty mornings when
you found absolutely nothing vanish from your memory. And you know
you'll be back next weekend. There are always more treasures."

Helie Robertson calls the sun porch her "southwestern corner." The carved pine bench with sun-bleached red paint and the Morris chair with original velvet upholstery were inexpensive flea-market trophies. "When we started collecting twenty years ago, no one wanted these and they were cheap. Prices have skyrocketed. Search hard and you can still find bargains, though," she said.

In the living room, an unsigned stained-glass lamp illuminates a tableau Robertson affectionately calls her "Indian kitsch" collection. Beaded moccasins, bookends, dolls, three birchbark canoes, bowls, and baskets were gathered in her travels through New Mexico.

Looking like an old Edward Curtis sepia print still life, Robertson's icons of the American West stand atop an old pine map cabinet. A tin canteen, Indian baskets, a birchbark canoe, antlers, an antique rug, and a storage jar displayed ensemble evoke a vanished era. The vintage stove works.

San Francisco interior designer Orlando Diaz-Azcuy is a man of strong opinions. Concerning the decoration of his country house near Bodega Bay he is quite clear: California "country" style doesn't have to dictate sun-faded colors, faux-rustic furniture, or European-country-themed design. ♦ The house is his escape from the city—the place where he often goes to work in solitude, but he wants no country cliches in the decor. Rather, his taste there runs to warm, intense colors, elegant antiques, and invigorating style...not so far afield from his city style. ♦ Orlando Diaz-Azcuy believes that the decor of country houses is usually limned for daytime and all too often addresses only the way the rooms will look and act in sunlight. ♦ "In my experience, everyone is outside or off on excursions during the day and hardly indoors at all," noted Diaz-Azcuy. "In reality, it's in the evening that everyone comes in for cocktails and for dinner. The paled-down tones and white and beige colors that most people choose for country houses look too washed-out and cold in the evening." ♦ On the California coast, fog quickly cools down the afternoon heat. Contrary to popular images of the West Coast's palmy nights, the end of the day is usually quite fresh. ♦ "I didn't want my house to be a mini-theater of warm-weather country style," said the designer, who was born in Cuba. "You can still have good antiques and quality fabrics—but not the finest antiques or silk. Practical cottons, good turn-of-the-century Louis XVI reproductions, and estate Biedermeier are perfect!"

Revved-up colors: For his country living room, San Francisco interior designer Orlando Diaz-Azcuy prefers colors with oomph rather than wishy-washy tones. The walls are white to showcase his sofas and a wing chair upholstered in terra-cotta-colored handwoven cotton. The Biedermeier-style occasional chair is upholstered in tan leather. Diaz-Azcuy improvised a pair of occasional tables from drum-shaped Japanese leather boxes. Firewood is stored in a New England basket.

Orlando Diaz-Azcuy bought his country house in 1991. ♦ "I had been looking for two years in the Napa Valley, but never found anything I liked. By chance, I was driving in the countryside beyond Sebastapol, near Freestone, and saw a sign," he said. The residence and an old barn were beautifully sited with a 360-degree view and mature trees—but the twenties house was a disaster. The modest exterior was painted barn red, the interiors a nightmarish magenta and blue. ♦ His plan for improving this country house was an exercise in quick, bold strokes—with little fuss or elaboration. He put in new oak plank floors and painted the exterior chocolate brown with black trim, to elide its ordinariness. ♦ "I started adding more and more color to the house and quickly realized that tones like warm terra-cotta, taupe, and sienna are needed so that the small rooms don't feel like a refrigerator at night," he said. ♦ To the mature bay trees, vintage apple trees, and Monterey pines on his three-acre property, he added twenty five liquidambar and fruitless mulberries, chestnut trees, and white and purple rhododendrons. Along the periphery of the lawn, and visible from the dining room, are banks of Spanish lavender.

No country cliches or sun-faded colors here: The walls of the dining room—used mostly for after-dark dinners— are painted warm terra-cotta. Diaz-Azcuy likes the provocative give-and-take of a three-tiered French chandelier above a very sculptural, very fifties Saarinen table with a marble top. His Louis XV–style chairs, formerly in a haute haute restaurant in San Francisco, were stripped of their overwrought gilding and pretentious red silk and painted pale gray. Muslin upholstery, gently worn, adds to the sense of imaginary heritage and the room's long-ago mood.

Light on two sides: Diaz-Azcuy added French doors to both of the bedrooms —so that he and his guests can snooze on cool linen sheets in hot afternoons and gaze out to the garden. The walls and ceilings of both bedrooms have been painted with faux striped canvas to look like Napoleonic campaign tents. (The painting was executed by The Master's Touch.) Here, too, the designer mixes simple, crisp fabrics and unpretentious antiques. In the green-striped bedroom he has placed a pair of almost-matching eighteenth-century Italian fruitwood chests of drawers. A pair of matching Biedermeier mirrors also give the room dimension. In the guest room, above, tall Casablanca lamps in gesso were designed by Orlando Diaz-Azcuy.

When Diaz-Azcuy purchased his Freestone house, the two bedrooms were small and somewhat banal. ◆ To give them architecture, better light, and distinction, he quickly added two pairs of French doors to each room, and had the walls and ceilings painted in lively stripes to look like a Napoleonic campaign tent. ◆ "At night, with up-lights illuminating the ceilings, the effect of a tent in the great outdoors is enhanced," the designer said. ◆ For light and temperature control the French doors also have wooden shutters. For added security they are closed when Diaz-Azcuy and his friends depart on Sunday evenings. ◆ At the back of the bedroom, which faces east, Diaz-Azcuy built a new fourteen-feet-by-thirty-feet deck with wide steps leading down to the lawn. For dining and reclining, he set out his relaxed Miami chairs (designed for HBF) slipcovered in washable white canvas. ◆ A pair of round wood columns installed on one side of the deck frames the vista of distant hills. The elegant columns and four large terra-cotta pots of white agapanthus also give a subtle sense of enclosure to friends sunbathing, reading, or chatting on the deck. ◆ Diaz-Azcuy has found the exercise of planning his Freestone house rather invigorating. He is now planning a new country retreat. This time, the interiors will be somewhat Modernist and very contemporary. ◆ "It will be a great experiment," said Diaz-Azcuy. "I think that as a designer I have a moral obligation to contribute to new ideas and fresh thinking for houses of today."

PEOPLE WHO LIVE ALONG THE CALIFORNIA COAST ARE DREAMERS. THEY HAVE TO BE. THERE IS PRECIOUS LITTLE

BUILDABLE LAND ALONG THIS ATTENUATED AND RUGGED GEOGRAPHY. ONLY A LIMITED NUMBER OF COASTAL PROPERTIES

OF GREAT CHARM AND GRACE EVER PUT OUT THE "FOR SALE" SIGN. AND TO FIND THEM AND CLAIM THEM REQUIRES IMAGI-

NATION, CLEVERNESS, DETERMINATION, AND LUCK. ♦ THE WORLD AT LARGE—AND FILMS AND TELEVISION—WOULD HAVE

US BELIEVE THAT MANY CALIFORNIANS LIVE IN BREEZY BEACH HOUSES. THEY IMAGINE CALIFORNIA LIVING AS A SPLASHY

DAVID HOCKNEY PAINTING. IN FACT, RELATIVELY FEW PEOPLE CAN STEP FROM THEIR DECK ONTO THE SAND, AND EVEN

FEWER CAN LIE IN BED AND WATCH A MARMALADE SUN SLIP BELOW THE HORIZON. ♦ IS THERE A VERNACULAR

CALIFORNIA COAST STYLE? HUNDREDS OF MILES OF BEACHES AND CLIFFS, AND CLIMATES RANGING FROM BALMY TO GRAY

AND FOGGY PRECLUDE THE POSSIBILITY OF "ONE SIZE FITS ALL." A LITTLE HOUSE ON THE BEACH NEAR DEL MAR OR IN

VENICE CAN BE ALL WINDOWS AND DOORS AND SUNNY TRANSPARENCY, BUT COTTAGES THAT TIPTOE ONTO THE

HEADLANDS OF MENDOCINO OR CLING TO THE MAJESTIC ROCKS OF BOLINAS OR BIG SUR SHOULD BE COSY AND WATER-

TIGHT, AND PREPARED FOR LASHINGS OF WINTER STORMS. ♦ THE BEST COASTAL HOUSES SUBMIT HAPPILY TO THE

LANDSCAPE. A SIMPLE BOARD-AND-BATTEN PAVILION POSES WITH GREAT PRESENCE AGAINST WINDSWEPT HEDGES OF PINE

AND FIR IN SEA RANCH. WEATHERED SHINGLES AND SOLID TIMBERS WERE ALSO CHOSEN BY JOHN DAVIS FOR HIS

STYLISH RE-DO OF A FIFTIES BEACH HOUSE IN STINSON BEACH. ♦ KIPP AND SHERNA STEWART LIVE ON A ROCKY OUTCROP

IN BIG SUR, WHERE THEY HAVE PATIENTLY AND WITH GREAT REVERENCE AND APPRECIATION REWORKED A HUMBLE

SHACK INTO A HOUSE OF GREAT WARMTH AND DISTINCTION. AND CORINNE WILEY, IN HER LANDMARK COTTAGE, TURNS

OFF THE RADIO SO THAT SHE CAN HEAR THE SLAP OF THE TIDE AND THE SCREECHING OF SEABIRDS. ♦ IN BOLINAS,

TIMOTHY MAXSON FOUND A WEEKEND HOUSE—WITH NO SOLID FOUNDATION—AND WILLED IT BACK TO LIFE. BENEATH

A FRAGRANT GROVE OF EUCALYPTUS, HE PLANTED A GARDEN OF LAVENDER, SALVIA, AND OLD ROSES. AND ABOVE

IT ALL IS HIS STUDIO—A FINE PLACE FOR WORKING AT HIS DESK, OR SIMPLY GAZING OUT TO SEA.

Kipp and Sherna Stewart's cottage is half hidden behind old native oaks and new Meyer lemon trees.
Their sight lines include more than thirty miles of the Big Sur coast and the ridges high above the surf.
The view will not disappear behind a new structure. Strictly enforced building restrictions ensure
that Big Sur can never be ruined. The few new houses permitted must be "out-of-site."

B
ig Sur is a mysterious, powerful, and historic region on the central California coast. ♦ Architectural designer Kipp Stewart and his wife, Sherna, a landscape designer, bought their house in Big Sur in 1972. From their kitchen windows they can see thirty miles down the coast. It's richly appointed now, but the house was originally somewhat primitive. ♦ Their house was sheltered by a noble stand of Coast live oaks, along with redwoods, tan oaks and madrones. Built first as a weekend cottage, its garden was simply a clearing in the bush beneath the trees. ♦ Over the last twenty-four years, the couple has thoughtfully, modestly, and with great respect refashioned their house and the landscape into a place of quiet beauty. ♦ The house, enlarged and improved gently over the years, suits the Stewarts well, and is now comfortably at home with its history. ♦ The garden—a series of stone stairways, terraces and sheltering hedges—feels out-of-time. Sherna Stewart's planting is sophisticated, shapely, and highly evolved. It's as if a protective conservancy has carefully guarded a stylish garden that had been planted there in the twenties. Except that there was no garden there in the twenties. ♦ "I'm influenced by the coast and the surrounding hillsides and this has been a long, slow process," said Sherna. "On trips to France or Spain or Italy, I would visit ancient gardens and study staircases, loggias, terraces, and hedges to see how they fashioned something simple, classic, and appropriate out of wilderness." ♦ "I had a very strong context in Big Sur. It's very challenging to start with raw landscape because when we moved here the land had no form or structure. There were no paths, no terraces—and any additions, sculpting, or reshaping had to be in the harmony with the surroundings."

Chamaecyparis, a conifer—along with pineapple guavas, palm trees, Meyer lemons, olives, and Italian cypresses—grow particularly well in the Stewarts' garden. Noble live oaks shelter the ridge and protect the other trees from fierce winter storms.

Room with a view: Kipp and Sherna Stewart's kitchen opens on one side to a deck and the Big Sur coast. Best of all, says Sherna, old Coast live oaks and shrubs frame the view and add to its allure.

The couple travel to Europe every year and are particularly fond of Italy. Roman pottery and Kipp's paintings are at home in the kitchen, but nothing upstages the landscape.

The Stewarts transformed the house and their gardens over twenty years. Working with simple materials such as terra-cotta pavers and stucco and keeping colors pellucid and minimal, they have crafted rooms that are cool and fresh in the summer and cheerful on cool, gray days. ◆ Big Sur has roof-rattling storms in winter, and fog rolls in on summer mornings. The house and garden, they knew, would have to feel right in a wide range of temperatures. ◆ "I've spent years building paths and moving out from the house a little at a time," said Sherna. "We've always followed the way the trees grow naturally. I never wanted to impose false and inappropriate form or materials here. I like to reveal the majesty of the natural setting." ◆ She planned vantage points and places to live in so that they could spend time in the garden. ◆ "With architecture, Kipp always likes to bring you into the best relationship with nature, the rising sun and the setting sun," noted Sherna. "I work that way, too. Now we have level patios sheltered by Meyer lemon trees and conifer hedges, so that we can bring a tea tray or dinner out and really live in the landscape. It's not our plan to domesticate the landscape, but rather to provide a poetic perch where we can contemplate and take in the view, the air, the breeze rustling the trees. Now we can visit and enjoy all four corners." ◆ The interior of the house— simple, uncluttered, refreshed through the seasons with nasturtiums or lemons from their garden—is now as the Stewarts like it. ◆ The garden will always be a work in progress. ◆ "I'm putting together a garden of proteas, which are very appropriate to the coast," said Sherna. "They come in a variety of subtle colors. Proteas are also drought tolerant, deer-proof, and do well among chaparral. They'll provide beautiful branches to bring into the house."

TIMOTHY MAXSON'S COTTAGE ON A HILLSIDE IN BOLINAS

Summer's sweetest memories always seem to involve sea breezes, seclusion, and sunny houses on the coast. ♦ Events consultant Timothy Maxson made his getaway from San Francisco nine years ago so that he could enjoy that carefree life all year ♦ "Living close to the beach, we can have the best of both worlds," said Maxson, who now shares the house with his partner, Don Smith. "It's less than an hour from the city over Mount Tamalpais. I had always loved coastal Marin and thought this would be the perfect escape route." ♦ Maxson loved the house and its eucalyptus-sheltered setting, and was not initially at all concerned that the foundation was crumbling and that Scottish broom and blackberry brambles had a stranglehold on the garden. ♦ After all, the afternoon sun was gilding the living room, westerly winds sighed in the trees, and peace had fallen on his soul. ♦ Maxson' research unearthed that his house had been built as a weekend cottage in 1924. ♦ "It had the most idyllic setting facing the water and nestled in the hillside," Maxson said. "I decided to take my time on the renovation. Instead of carpentry, I went into gardening with a passion." ♦ He had his land bulldozed into terraces, built new paths with river rocks, and began planting vegetables, shrubs, and flowers. Pathways are now fragrant with old roses and French lavender. Ornamental grasses, verbascum, and plants such as New Zealand flax that flourish with little water wave in a gentle breeze. Artichokes, herbs, and lettuces are cultivated in a sunny patch near the kitchen window.

Events consultant Timothy Maxson took two years to renovate his nine hundred square foot shingled house near the Marin coast. Every day he cultivates his colorful, fragrant garden. It's green year-round on his hillside. Winter in Bolinas is brief, and spring blooms often open in February. The residence is tiny, with just one bedroom, so Maxson and Smith keep the rooms airy and uncluttered. A large Kreiss sofa with wool twill upholstery anchors the living room. His coffee table and corner table are hand-painted.

Timothy Maxson, who loves to cook and entertain, built a new sky-lit kitchen. Counter tiles were handcrafted in Mexico. On wide counters, he sets out cool drinks and salads for ravenous friends returning from long beach hikes.

Three years ago, Maxson finally began his remodel in earnest. He replaced the house's old foundation and installed new plumbing, new wiring, and new floors. His biggest project was a new kitchen. ♦ "The kitchen was important to me because I love to cook," said Maxson, a former caterer. "I wanted large windows and lots of light, plus views of the garden." ♦ He pushed the back wall out three-and-a-half feet, and installed a new gabled roof with a two-and-a-half-by-four-foot skylight. ♦ "The new kitchen design is a metaphor for seaside entertaining," he said. "It is open, relaxed, colorful and very accessible." ♦ With a large sink, two wide counters topped with aqua-colored ceramic tiles, and a restaurant-style stove, the kitchen makes light work of weekend entertaining. ♦ "We set out all the vegetables, salad greens, and other ingredients for lunch and get my friends to work rinsing and chopping," laughed Maxson. ♦ He was surprised to discover that he enjoys winter near the coast as much as summer. ♦ "Winter here is generally very mild. It rains, and it's often misty, but I can garden or go walking on the beach most days," he said. ♦ "We plan to stay here for a long time," Maxson said. "Having a house and garden is a long-term commitment. I just planted an Italian stone pine that won't look its best for another thirty years."

Timothy Maxson's studio/office, with its view of the Marin County coast.

Maxson's intention was to keep his living room/dining room almost monochromatic—the better to play up the coastal view. The old fireplace was original to the house. A dining table with a natural canvas cloth is set up in one corner of the room.

Thirty-two years ago, San Francisco architect William Turnbull Jr was one of the original designers of Sea Ranch, a carefully planned coastal community three hours north of San Francisco. There, simple shingled structures, their shapes and detailing inspired by indigenous old barns and farmhouses, stand in grassy meadows. Beyond wind-tossed cypress windbreaks and fields of wildflowers and lupines, winter gales rage at sea, and the sun slips below the horizon with magnificent finality. ◆ Houses at Sea Ranch make special demands. They must have walls of glass to welcome vistas, and wood-paneled rooms that shelter against storms and cool down summer's warmth. ◆ Ed and Kathleen Anderson had wanted a retreat and a place that would welcome friends. ◆ "I built this house to display the view which is in turn moody, barren, and magnificent," said Turnbull. He devised an L-shaped plan that deflects northwest winds but brings the coast view into every room. ◆ "The Douglas fir walls and ceilings and exposed rafters create warmth and comfort, like a protective shell," said Turnbull's associate, Eric Haesloop. "We paid a lot of attention to every detail, so that the interior of the house feels like a finely crafted cabinet."

The cedar-shingled house in a Sea Ranch meadow stands open to sky and sea views. It's the perfect alliance of architecture and nature. An 18-foot long window seat wraps around the living room's corner windows, offering a broad, pillowed spot for reading. Here guests watch summer fog creep across the silent meadows and whales spouting in the ocean beyond. No window coverings intervene, so nature's drama seems hardly separate from the quiet calm of the Douglas-fir-paneled rooms.

CORINNE WILEY'S HOUSE ON BELVEDERE COVE

Interior designer Corinne Wiley keeps an old wooden dory and a Sunfish on her dock and often sails or rows out into Belvedere Cove. But one suspects that it is not primarily the pleasures of venturing through the sheltered waters that drew her to her waterfront cottage in Belvedere fifteen years ago. ♦ It's the house that holds her in thrall. One of five originally built as luxurious guest cottages for the adjacent Belvedere Hotel, they were saved when the hotel was torn down in the twenties to make way for the San Francisco Yacht Club. ♦ "These cottages were designed and built by architect Albert Farr, in 1894, and I think they're better today than ever," Wiley enthused. "They're not large, but they have a generous spirit and sense of welcome." ♦ The weathered-timber house, in the First Bay Tradition, takes elements from Shingle Style, Early American houses, Early Medieval architecture—with a Swiss chalet detail or two. Beneath the black-painted eaves on the side facing the cove, there's a carving of shrouded nuns. Still, the skillful and witty architect avoided mere pastiche. The house feels cohesive—very much itself. ♦ The small entry garden leads to a broad foyer. Downstairs, there is a living room, a dining room, and a sunny kitchen. There are three ratherfanciful bedrooms upstairs under the eaves. Two have extravagantly swagged *lits a la polonaises*. ♦ "The waterfront deck is my year-round favorite room," said Wiley. Sheltered on three sides, it has an up-close view of Belvedere Cove. Across a forest of masts in the yacht harbor Wiley can view the tall towers of downtown San Francisco—if it's not foggy.

On her waterfront deck overlooking Belvedere Cove, Corinne Wiley sets out a dining table and French iron chairs. An old-fashioned lawn swing upholstered in weatherproof canvas is a fresh-air spot for a post-prandial nap. On a clear day, Wiley can view San Francisco Bay beyond the marina. The cottage—and the other four in the row—was given into historic preservation in 1994 and now little can be changed inside or out except to upgrade kitchens and bathrooms.

"I rarely turn on the radio," said Wiley. "I listen to waves breaking under the house, the tide going in and out, birds talking to each other, foghorns, riggings rattling in the wind, and the docks clanging, creaking and groaning." ♦ It's a very bewitching house. "If I'm entertaining I have only candlelight," Wiley said. "You can see all the lights on the docks and reflections flickering on the water. Sometimes, the city lights across the water glow as bright as diamonds." ♦ The house is a home base for an international roster of friends—as well as Wiley's grandchildren. ♦ "I didn't want to have shades on the windows, and the sun pours in most days," said the designer. "I chose neutral colors such as taupe, beige, pale apricot, and pale blue, so that I wouldn't have to worry about fabrics fading." ♦ She has chosen luxurious fabrics but used them in a very off-hand way. Her sofa is in off-white silk chenille, with Fortuny pillows. A window banquette is cream silk velvet. ♦ This is the home of a traveler— and a knowledgeable collector. Wiley has a fanciful carved Venetian occasional table in the dining room, an English chinoiserie cabinet with French boxes and mirrors in the sitting room, and nineteenth-century landscape and seascape paintings near the entry that draw the viewer into scenes of long-ago idyllic settings. ♦ "I didn't want the decorating to be too stiff," she said. "I think of it as an enchanted cottage. It's inspiring. I have so many ideas when I just sit quietly here."

Wiley's house is a very privileged spot from which to view the changing tides, sunlight glimmering on the cove, sails propelled by zephyrs, and curious birds that flutter and dart about her deck. She often sets up a weekend buffet in the dining room so that guests may dine on the deck, or find a cosseted spot beside a window.

In a corner of her living room, a Louis Philippe gold-leaf mirror hangs above an eighteenth-century fruitwood commode with ormolu pulls. The lantern is from Venice. "Everything is small-scale because it's a small house," said Wiley.

A Venetian blackamoor with a carved, feather skirt stands before mirrored French doors in the dining

room. A simple French tone-on-tone cotton print on the dining table is draped with an old silk obi sash.

The dining chairs are Louis Quinze-style, and the painted cabriole-leg table is Venetian. Wiley is

rather partial to Venetian furniture. It is fanciful and less serious than some French furniture, she said.

Designer John Davis bought his house within sound of the ocean at Stinson Beach in 1993 after searching for two years. He knew he would have to up-date and redesign the small "very fifties" bungalow. ♦ "At a popular place like Stinson Beach, where very few houses are ever on the market, you have to make do with what's available," said Davis, who had been living in Sausalito for twenty years. ♦ Stinson Beach, just north of San Francisco, is considered the prime real estate location along the north coast because it is virtually the only town with ocean, lagoon, and beach front properties. ♦ The I-bedroom house had inappropriate picture windows, dark plywood walls, brown asphalt tile floors, and one meager tree. ♦ "It was a great challenge to make such a modest structure look elegant," Davis said. ♦ Working with contractor/carpenter James Lino, Davis first built a six-foot high redwood fence for privacy and shelter from the wind. He planted boxwood, maple trees, jasmine, and white hydrangeas so that the garden would be well on its way when the house was completed four months later. ♦ "I liked the basic strength and simplicity of my house," said Davis. "The timber construction had integrity and strength. I had to redesign the interior to give it style and grace." ♦ For four months Davis and James Lino worked to remove interior walls and open up the house to its new enclosed garden. Lino built French doors in the front living room and in the kitchen to afford views of the verdant surroundings. ♦ "I followed the Japanese theory of creating your own retreat with private views over the garden," said Davis. "The house is only twenty-four feet by thirty-five feet. Now when I open the French doors on sunny days it feels much bigger." ♦ Davis designed a new living room/dining room, with a handsome brick fireplace topped with an overscale oiled-redwood mantel. ♦ The walls of the Crafstman-style interior were painted with Pompeii Red and Carnation Pink paints (subtler than they sound) from Paint Magic. That's the only splash of color. Davis kept furniture bold in scale and neutral in color. His black-painted circular dining table serves for entertaining and as a useful work table.

Designer John Davis and James Lino worked together to give the house as much fine craftsmanship as they could. Tall gates and fences guard privacy. Bronze hardware on the custom French doors, new redwood ceiling beams and the finely carved mantel make the small house rich in detail. Floor-to-ceiling mirrors enlarge the apparent space and reflect endlessly. On a sheltered terrace, Davis can relax on painted deck chairs.

THOSE FORTUNATE TO HAVE DRIVEN NORTH ALONG THE WINDING SILVERADO TRAIL, OR THROUGH THE VINEYARDS

JUST OUTSIDE SONOMA OR SANTA YNEZ, HAVE PROBABLY GLANCED OUT INTO THE FIELDS OR UP AMONG THE

MADRONES AND IMAGINED THEIR OWN HOUSE THERE. ♦ THE CALIFORNIA WINE COUNTRY, WHICH SLEPT IN RURAL BLISS

FOR A HUNDRED YEARS OR SO, HAS BECOME A FAVORITE OF CITY DWELLERS. SOME ARE REMODELING NEGLECTED

COTTAGES AND PLANTING NEW GARDENS, OTHERS ARE DECORATING FOR WARM-WEATHER RELAXATION. ♦ THESE ARE

HOSPITABLE HOUSES THAT EMBRACE OWNERS AND GUESTS ALIKE WITH OPEN ARMS. THEY DON'T STAND ON

CEREMONY. ♦ IN NORTHERN AND SOUTHERN WINE-GROWING REGIONS, SUMMERS ARE USUALLY HOT AND DRY, AND

WINTERS ARE COOLER, OCCASIONALLY GRAY AND DAMP. FOR THE TURNING SEASONS, HOUSES THERE MUST

OFFER QUIET CORNERS, SHADED GARDENS FOR ALFRESCO LUNCHES IN THE SUMMER, AND HEARTY HEARTHS FOR WINTER

AFTERNOON SNOOZING. ♦ TRUE TO THEIR OWN IDEALS OF SPONTANEITY AND EXPERIMENTATION, JEAN AND

CHUCK THOMPSON SEE THEIR SONOMA INTERIORS ALMOST AS A LABORATORY. FABRICS ARE TRIED, NEW PAINTINGS ARE

BROUGHT IN, A FRESH WALL PAINT IS CONSIDERED. ♦ RICHARD CRISMAN AND JEFF BROCK, FORTUNATE IN

FRIENDSHIPS, HAD THEIR CHUMS' HELP WITH SETTING UP THEIR YOUNTVILLE WEEKEND HOUSE. AN AUSTERE "CONTRAC-

TOR SPECIAL" WAS THEIR POINT OF DEPARTURE. NOW, ROSES BLOOM IN THE GARDEN, LIVING ROOM SOFAS

COMFORT GUESTS RETURNING FROM ST. HELENA ANTIQUES EXPEDITIONS, AND THE ALL-WHITE KITCHEN INVITES EVERY-

ONE TO COME IN AND COOK. ♦ STEPHEN SHUBEL, WITH GREAT ENCOURAGEMENT FROM HIS CLIENTS STEVE SILVER AND

JO SHUMAN SILVER, WOKE UP A SLEEPY LITTLE COTTAGE WITH COLORS OF COUNTRY MEADOW FLOWERS.

Like Northern California pioneers a hundred years before, Ron Mann
and Louise La Palme Mann took on the challenge of making gardens on rocky,
unpromising terrain. On their Sonoma terrace, he designed the Douglas Fir
daybed, she handprinted the fabrics.

Charles and Jean Thompson, Pacific Heights residents during the week, have dared to reinvent "city dwellers go to the country."

Their free-spirited and exploratory approach to relaxed country style melds custom-designed furniture and flea market trophies, funky and fine

vintage Mexican folk arts, hothouse and hedgerow flowers, and a burgeoning collection of paintings by emerging artists on both sides

of the border. ♦ "We're inventing our rooms as we go along," said Jean blithely. "We began with non-statement things like ticking-upholstered

sofas and stone lamps and have added and up-graded as we went along." ♦ Thanks to trips to the Mexican hill towns and their

friendship with Ron and Louise Mann, the decor has become bolder and more colorful. The couple has leap-frogged over the initial stylish-

but-quiet design into sunny yellow, bold sienna, umber, turquoise, and vibrant, happy clashes of Mexican pinks, reds and greens. ♦ "We bought

the house in 1989 for occasional use in the summer, but we're going there more and more often, and plan to move there permanently

soon," said Jean, a partner with Barbara Belloli in Fioridella, one of San Francisco's top flower shops. ♦ Perhaps the boldest change to the

1,600 square foot house was a recent remodel, which transformed a former central deck into a skylit solarium. ♦ The room, adjacent

to the dining area, is furnished with armless fifties sofas, an Indian silver chair, and a mismatched collection of tables. Here, the Thompsons

gather in the evening for cocktails, or on Sunday morning to read the newspaper.

"This is a small house, so it's important to be able to use it all," said Chuck
Thompson. In refashioning a former open deck into an enclosed, sky-lit solarium,
the Thompsons dramatically changed the whole house. The sunny new room
has become a vibrant center, with vintage sofas refreshed with canvas slipcovers
and a wire jar lamp by Ron Mann. The silver chair is from Rajastan.
The Thompsons found the old barred window frame in Mexico and added the
mirror to suggest a real window.

The sculptural, wedge-shaped yellow dining table was custom-made for the Thompsons by their friend, interior designer Ron Mann. On it Jean arranges Mexican majolica candle-holders and pitchers, along with 'Cecile Brunner' roses from the garden and tulips in a faux Aalto vase in terra-cotta. Indonesian chairs are from the Ginsberg Collection. The two curvy politically correct—maple plywood Knoll chairs are by architect Frank Gehry. "They work very well here because they're very compact and vertical," said Chuck.

"You can see the garden from every room now, so the house never feels tiny or claustrophobic," noted Jean. "In the summer we leave the doors open so that the scent of 'Cecile Brunner' roses or jasmine or Casablanca lilies fills the room. At nightfall, the fragrance is very intense and we feel as if we're in the middle of a flower garden." ◆ The couple has turned up the volume on color over the years, but they have left the walls white. ◆ "We have so much texture and color going on that we like to leave the walls pale — but I wouldn't be surprised if I added more color there," Jean said. ◆ Mexican village pottery with the dusty patina of age, rusted Cor-Ten steel sculptures by Ron Mann, and sofas upholstered in Louise La Palme Mann's handpainted cottons are part Thompson-style, part "Don't make hard work of the weekend" ethic. ◆ "Our paintings, the Mexican hand-carved furniture, and our collections are souvenirs in the best sense. They recall meetings with the artists, an antique shop we fell upon in Oaxaca or Mexico City, Christmas in Puerto Vallarta. They're full of meaning to us," said Jean. "Once we bring a vintage toy truck, a silver vase, or a clay candelabra home, they become part of our lives. In the city or in Sonoma, they make us feel at home."

The Thompsons have always liked one-of-a-kind furniture and take great pleasure in finding emerging painters and craftspeople. ♦ Over the years they have commissioned Sonoma designer Ron Mann to design for them Cor-Ten steel tables, a yellow dining table, a pair of wire jar lamps, and a stone-column standard lamp. ♦ Now they're also working closely with fabric designer Louise La Palme Mann, who has made cut-work pillows, shower curtains, handsome handmade quilted throws with leather appliques, and new hand-painted slipcovers for the sofas. ♦ "We love Mexican crafts, too, because there is a lot of heart in the work," mused Jean. "We've got angel faces, Day of the Dead skeletons, pottery from Oaxaca, old terracotta dinnerware from Puebla, and platters from Morelia. When Chuck and I take trips to Puerto Vallarta, the beach vendors with interesting things always seem to appear in front of us." ♦ Still, thanks to their well-edited displays, their house never looks like, "my trip to Mexico." ♦ "We're always looking for pieces that have whimsy, spirit and spontaneity," Chuck said. "Fine craftsmanship is important, but what's really thrilling is the sense of ecstasy in the work by village artists."

Large-scale furniture and a tall rusted iron mirror from the Ginsberg Collection give the small living room an authoritative, spacious air. The windows and doors are left uncovered to get the full effect of Sonoma's summer sunshine. On a vintage pine dresser, the Thompsons cluster a collection of Mexican paintings, retablos, antique toys, pottery vases, and garden flowers.
"We get the most pleasure from honestly made country-artisan pieces that are not precious," said Jean, who has mastered the art of shipping vintage bowls and fragile pots from Guanajuato, Puerto Angel, San Miguel Allende, Palenque, Zacatecas, or Puerto Vallarta, always trusting that a beach or outdoor market vendor's wares will make a safe journey home to San Francisco. The lamp with the beaded-glass shade is from Limn.

The Thompsons' country garden is quite small, but Chuck keeps it flourishing all year. In Spring great pink clouds of 'Cecile Brunner' roses bank over their fence. Foxgloves, agapanthus, Casablanca lilies, hydrangeas, flax, and lavender all do well in the hot dry summer and cool foggy winter.

RON MANN & LOUISE LA PALME MANN'S GARDEN IN SONOMA

Country properties can be a blessing—and a problem waiting to be solved. They seldom land in your lap perfect in every way.

Houses on the market are usually dated or kitschy, and gardens have often been neglected. Sometimes the picturesque farm buildings that shelter

beneath old trees are within a foggy day of falling down. ♦ Interior designer Ron Mann started out with high hopes. In 1989,

soon after he and his wife, Louise, were married in Majorca, he bought ten acres with an old barn in the middle of an extinct volcano crater

north of the quiet town of Sonoma. Great rocky outcrops give the landscape its noble, timeless quality. ♦ "We took possession of

our property on Thanksgiving Day," Mann recalled. "It was unusually chilly. We wrapped ourselves warmly, sat there in a weed patch, ate our

turkey, and gave thanks." ♦ But the dream faltered the minute Ron first jabbed a garden spade into the soil. ♦ "I quickly realized that

you can't dig here. Our whole plateau is stone. It's all volcanic rock—the ones you can see and many more lurking under the surface. There's no

real soil for plants to grow in," Ron Mann said. Still, they were determined to grow sunflowers, vegetables, herbs, and lavender. ♦ Noted

stonemason Jeronimo Perez started constructing walls with stones from the property. Working in a traditional dry-wall, no-mortar

method from his native Mexico, he stacked stones to make sculptural and very practical walls. On hardscrabble outcrops and beneath magnifi-

cent old oaks, he laid terraces that have given form and great beauty to the unpromising garden. ♦ Perez quarries the stones on a

Ron Mann and Jeronimo Perez used all the old wood on the property to reconstruct
the old barn. The exterior walls are all recycled timber. In the shade of the old barn, Ron
Mann's sunflower-yellow high-back Douglas fir-plank chairs are a jolt of color and
geometry. The old shutters are from Majorca. He is a master of shaping simple, powerful
still lifes from objets trouvés. Rocks, old bottles, rusted implements and handfuls of weeds are
his inspiration here. Perez crafted the terrace, steps, paths and garden walls using volcanic
rocks from an old quarry on the property.

In the herb garden, Louise La Palme Mann planted a fragrant knot garden using chives, oregano, lemon verbena, caraway thyme, pineapple sage, and golden marjoram. Stone walls shelter the tender leaves from afternoon breezes. Mann planned the flower garden carefully—to look impromptu and wild. Favorite blue flowers— verbena, salvia, clary sage—wind their stems among lemon balm and golden yarrow. Beauty is evanescent. Soon after the yellow Mexican primroses were photographed, discriminating deer munched them for lunch.

far corner of the land. Terraces now surround the house, and stone walls protect Louise's herb and flower gardens from fierce afternoon winds and scorching summer sun. ◆ "It's all structure now, and we never fret that we can't grow roses or plan lawns or plant bulbs in this soil," said Mann. ◆ The Manns have worked long days transforming their land. Fields of lavender are visible from the front door. They have built Douglas-fir sofas and massive recycled wood tables so that they can dine and repose on the new shady terraces. ◆ The barn, too, was initially a disappointment, and several friends told Mann to tear it down. ◆ "If we had leaned on the barn it would have fallen down," recalled Mann. Working with Perez, he gathered up all of the old wood on the property and set about refastening the barn to its foundations. The recycled wood now supports the barn, and was used to fashion handsome (and secure) exterior walls. ◆ The rugged walls and graceful terraced look as if they have been on the property for centuries . . . not two years. ◆ "Friends who were at our wedding in Deia say the stone work reminds them of Majorca," Ron Mann said. "It's the highest compliment."

Louise La Palme Mann has gained recognition in the decorating world as a designer of bold hand-printed cotton fabrics. Now she's letting her talent as a gardener blossom. Undaunted by adobe soil, wild winds that whip across the property in the late afternoons, and intense Sonoma sunshine, she has patiently nurtured herb and flower gardens of transcendent beauty. Hers is a model for an easy-care country garden. Chosen for their grace and ability to fend for themselves, her plants are also fragrant and flavorful. ♦ After three years of experimentation and some disappointments, she has given up on roses, hollyhocks, coreopsis, and Mexican primroses. Neighborhood deer, picturesque at a distance, nip off their tender buds. ♦ "First we built up the stone walls for shelter and structure, then I topped up the soil with more than two feet of new soil, manure and mushroom compost," she said. "The soil is everything for a serious gardener! I installed a drip watering system. I can't water every day and the heat is intense and very drying in summer." ♦ She made two gardens for herbs and flowers, and planted two large fields of lavender. Near the house is Lavandula 'Grosso,' which has deep blue/purple flowers. Beyond the stone driveway are the undulating bushes of Lavandula intermedia 'Provence,' one of the most fragrant of lavenders. The valley climate here is particularly suited for lavender.

The garden changes dramatically with each month. In January, fresh green growth carpets the meadows. By April, the lavender is verdant and budding, and native California poppies open their orange faces to the sun. The summer brings sunflowers. By fall, colors are muted and the fields are sere.

RICHARD CRISMAN & JEFF BROCK'S RETREAT IN YOUNTVILLE

Richard Crisman and Jeff Brock's house in the Napa Valley is truly a *maison d'amis.* ♦ Their chums Stephanie Mayer, Dennis Leggett, Stephen Brady, and Karen Nicks all helped design, decorate, and style the interiors—and any weekend the rooms and garden resound with sun-struck hilarity and arrivals and departures. ♦ When Crisman and Brock are away on business, friends make the one-hour drive north to Yountville to bask in the sheltered garden and water the roses. And there's always their best friend, Kennedy the gold Labrador, a faithful companion. ♦ "We found the house four years ago after we'd given up on finding a house we could afford in San Francisco," said Crisman, VP of advertising and public relations for Gap. Brock is a real estate advisor. ♦ "Every weekend we'd go looking for a house to buy, and we got farther and farther from the city," Brock recalled. ♦ Finally, Crisman's mother discovered the house hidden away on a quiet cul-de-sac in Yountville. Contractor-built, it was on a "flag" lot behind other houses, but with a well-designed swimming pool and the makings of a garden. ♦ "It was the perfect, manageable size and very private," noted Crisman. "We could arrive on Friday night, stock the refrigerator, mow the lawn, water the garden, and then relax."

Jeff Brock said he did not know he had a green thumb until he started gardening at their weekend house. The pool terrace and beds around the house bloom with lavender, poppies, and jasmine. Brock's favorite roses which thrive in the Napa summer: 'Chicago Peace,' 'Mister Lincoln,' 'Just Joey,' 'White Lightening,' 'Chrysler Imperial,' 'Broadway,' and 'Iceberg.' The chaises longues are from Smith & Hawken.

The fifties French garden table makes a neat nest for garden roses. A sunny spot for Saturday morning newspaper reading, the window seat has denim pillows.

The pale terra-cotta stucco house with white trim was new and somewhat bland at first sight. ♦ "We worked fast to give it instant character and a feeling of some history—even though it was brand-new," recalled Crisman. ♦ They added French doors, painted the kitchen white, and began to lay out the rose beds. Antiques and old garden furniture gave the rooms personality. ♦ "We like to keep the decor loose and fun," Crisman said. "You don't want to spend the weekend straightening everything, so we chose neutral, simple colors and natural fabrics with interesting textures. The furniture is overscale and we've got just what we need —no clutter." ♦ Much of any summer weekend is spent outdoors. They make fast forays to valley farmers' markets and vegetable stands, and set up lunch on a teak table under a large canvas umbrella. ♦ "We follow the sun," Crisman said. "The sun rises on the swimming pool side, then we may go indoors to make lunch. As the sun sets over the hills to the west, we take dinner out in the front garden." ♦ The house takes the seasons in stride. In the late autumn, with French doors closed and a log fire glowing, the living room sofas are cloaked with cashmere throws. Down-filled pillows and kilim rugs add comfort and cheer. ♦ "We don't close the house for winter," Crisman noted. "We sit around the fire in December, and usually by January and February the weather starts to brighten. It's very much a year-round house."

Deep, lingering relaxation is encouraged by overstuffed armchairs and sofas from Shabby Chic. Slipcovers are beige linen and white denim—all easily washed. Pillows are by Polo Ralph Lauren. The old pine coffee table—great for winter board games and setting up summer snacks—is from Bale Mill Classic Country Furniture just north of St. Helena.

The white-painted bookshelves were original to the house. Crisman and Brock arranged tableaux with framed photos, gardening volumes, Paris flea market finds, vases and candles. One favorite memento: a dried sunflower from their first summer at the house.

One reason the Napa Valley is popular with busy San Franciscans is that the summer heat induces indolence. Still, there are mecca restaurants like The French Laundry in Yountville for chic, worldly fare. And when the mood strikes Crisman and Brock for a rather formal Saturday night feast, their dining room is all urbane polish and comfort. Crisman and Brock furnished from sources in the city and in the valley. The table, a tracery of iron curves, is from Bale Mill Classic Country Furniture.

Dining chairs are by McGuire. The side table is from George V in San Francisco. Favorite framed photos include works by Duane Michals, Mark Klett, Diane Arbus, and William Wegman. Terra-cotta pavers were a practical choice for the front entry. The pine chest is an old garage-sale find. Sculptural and very comfortable, the metal garden chair can be taken out to the terrace.

The bedrooms at Crisman and Brock's house were by no means an afterthought. Not for them

the hand-me-downs of other weekend houses. In the large, sunfilled main bedroom, an antique pine bed

is piled with luxurious linens from Sue Fisher King. Orchids and garden roses grace tables.

Flowers, books, and a vintage etching draw the eye.

In a house with pale, creamy tones, the red bedroom stands out. On the antique painted Russian-

style bed from Sue Fisher King, they've arranged linens by Polo Ralph Lauren. The patterned cottons,

along with an oil portrait and banks of pillows, give the small room both a feeling of ease

and distinct character.

TOM & LINDA SCHEIBAL'S LOG HOUSE IN ST. HELENA

A log house is not exactly common in the Napa Valley. Tom and Linda Scheibal's house, built on a hillside north of St. Helena in 1979 from a Maine kit, was probably the first. ♦ The house may be singular, but it is very much at home in the valley. Surrounded by firs, antique apple trees, and old pines, it looks much as it would in the Maine backwoods—except that it has a fine view of vineyards and gnarled vines growing in dusty red clay. ♦ "In the late seventies, when I had an antique shop in San Francisco, I often made trips to small-town Maine," recalled Tom. "I found very pure American antiques that I shipped back to my Powell Street shop. On my forays, I would also see these stout little log houses. They seemed very airtight and solid—warm in the winter and cool and shady in summer. I wanted one." ♦ In 1979, just after he purchased an acre of land next to a state park between St. Helena and Calistoga, Scheibal discovered the North-Eastern Logs company, which offered log cabin design services and a 2,000-square-foot "kit" house for $14,000. ♦ "That low price was amazing, even in the late seventies," admitted Tom. "I then spent $3,000 to ship the logs across country from Maine to the California coast. They were originally a bargain, and even by the time I got them to St. Helena and had a contractor put the kit together, it cost less than $100,000." ♦ More significantly, Scheibal and his contractors had to walk each of the hundreds of logs—all numbered—up the hill to the site. The house was assembled log by log. ♦ "I had to deal with picky building inspectors who had never dealt with log construction before," he remembered. ♦ The interior of the house had been milled to create a flat tongue-in-groove surface. ♦ "We had the interior walls smoothed out because all that loggy stuff looks too 'frontier village' and too bumpy," said Scheibal, who has three wine-country stores selling furniture and accessories.

In summer, the exterior of the Scheibals' log house is barely visible beneath a pink froth of 'Cecile Brunner' roses, old crab apple trees, and a tangle of jasmine and honey-suckle vines. The greenery curtains their wide verandah, where they stay cool on summer afternoons. The antique wicker table, sofa, and chairs are from Bar Harbor, Maine. In summer, the family takes breakfast here, to watch the sun come up across the valley.

The two-story house with dormers has a large, wide shaded porch that wraps around two sides. ♦ Scheibal added interior walls to delineate a large living room with an iron fireplace, a sunny music room, a dining room overlooking the valley, a large kitchen, and three petite bedrooms. ♦ "Over the years the logs seemed to get darker and darker, and the house felt very woodsy," observed Scheibal. His next step was to whitewash the walls to brighten the interior. The dark floors were bleached. ♦ In 1982, he married Linda, a music teacher, and they now have two music-loving daughters, Meggie and Blaire. ♦ "We often wonder why this log house works so well in the valley, because it's not exactly an indigenous style," mused Scheibal. "If it were standing in the middle of a vineyard with no trees, it would be all wrong. But it's built on a hillside surrounded by pines and gnarled apple trees, and it looks quite Maine-ish." ♦ The couple started out with fine Maine antiques. With white walls and pale floors for contrast, the antiques came alive. ♦ "I never wanted the rooms to look Maine-cottage themed," said Scheibal. "That gets old fast."

Hickory wing chairs wear their gray-and-white linen slipcovers and mustard-painted legs with bravado. The glass-topped table was designed by Diego Giacometti. The black-and-white ceramic vase is by Sandy Simon. Clearly, the Scheibals are not willing to submit themselves to one theme. Instead, they take the somewhat more difficult route to combining antiques with contemporary furniture, vintage Maine finds, and new California crafts.

The couple has paintings by California artists such as Roy de Forest and Wade Hoefer. Their newest trophy is a sofa upholstered in mustard-yellow leather. Bringing in contemporary style kick-starts rooms with antiques and makes the decor look less precious, more livable. ◆ The ceiling in the living room is double-height, which keeps the house cool in summer. It also provides excellent acoustics for the harpsichord, their piano, plus recorder, cello, and violin recitals by the Scheibal ensemble. ◆ At Christmas, the house comes alive. They decorate a tree and bring out a collection of antique music boxes. The house feels snug and cozy. ◆ The weather there is very seasonal. Summers are hot, but it's normal to see frost on the ground, and snow every few years. The house handles all of this with ease. ◆ "I originally built the house for myself and my son, Quinn," noted Scheibal. "Then I married Linda and we had the girls. This house has so exceeded any idea I originally had about it. It was clearly the best investment."

Let music ring: The parents, Meggie, and Blaire gather around the grand piano in the music room to make wonderful and passionate music. The Maine secretary stores books and sheet music. Scheibal's collection of framed nautical paintings, a carved fish decoy, ships in bottles, and San Francisco scenes hang on the wall. "I'm from the Pacific Northwest, and I've always had a great love of boats," he said. He also lived among old fishing families in San Francisco's North Beach and found many maritime paintings and trophies there.

Antique French posters, vintage enameled cola signs, and a pair of carnival wheels from Maine

are the zap! of primary colors on the white-washed plank walls. The floor is travertine marble tiles.

The Scheibals topped their counters with practical galvanized steel. The cupboard fronts are steel

grating, for a jelly-cupboard effect.

S ummers in San Francisco are cool, gray, and often foggy, as even the most ardent fan of the City by the Bay will admit. And so it was that twelve years ago, impresario Steve Silver purchased a twenties house in Sonoma to assure himself and his fiancée, Jo Schuman, and their friends of weekend sunshine. ◆ The half-acre property was beautifully located on a quiet street just off the historic town square. Lemon and orange trees flourished in the garden. ◆ Their 1,000-square-foot house was tiny but full of potential. It boasted two bedrooms, a living room and a neat kitchen—just enough space for a relaxing respite from Beach Blanket Babylon, Steve Silver's long-running, hit show. ◆ Silver decorated the house simply, at first with the help of Gary Hutton, and enjoyed it for a few years before renting it out to friends. Two years ago, he returned to the house and wanted to spiff up the property and give it a dash of style. ◆ "Steve wanted his little house to be luxurious, but casual and very comfortable," said Jo Schuman Silver, his widow. ◆ The Silvers commissioned interior designer Stephen Shubel to fashion elegant interiors for their retreat. ◆ "The house was a little tattered, and except for a white-lacquered dining table and a pair of plinths, we were starting from scratch," said Shubel, known for his relaxed and chic decor. ◆ "My idea was to do the interiors in shades of periwinkle blue," he said. ◆ Periwinkle became the signature hue. This classic color of summer meadow flowers seems to tame the afternoon's torpor and send a signal to the brain, "Relax!"

Jo Schuman Silver's weekend house has a flower-filled front garden. Decorator Stephen Shubel selected cool, soothing Oxford cloth in periwinkle and cornflower blue striped with ivory for the armchairs and sofa in the living room. (Fabrics by Rela Gleason for Summer Hill.) For extra zip, the tailored upholstery is piped in white cotton. The ottoman—a versatile addition to a relaxed room—is covered in deep periwinkle-blue cotton chenille by Glant. Buttons and piping are white denim. Draperies are vanilla linen. Walls are painted pale blue 'Atmosphere' by Fuller-O'Brien. Roses throughout the house are from Silver's garden.

The plan for the Silvers' cottage was to keep the decorating uncomplicated, fresh, and very functional. Still, Shubel brought the rooms a high degree of sophistication and detail. ♦ Down-filled sofas and chairs in the living room are superbly tailored, with crisp white piping and contrast buttons. ♦ "Lots of fabric, pounds of down, and glossy white woodwork give country cottages glamor that's not too citified," noted Shubel. By using one color in several variations he kept the rooms from looking gaudy or overdone. ♦ "Steve's collection of blue-and-white antique porcelain bowls, boxes, jars, plates, and urns was a great inspiration for the color scheme," said Shubel. ♦ The porcelain, unusual in country houses in California, is showcased on the mantel and on occasional tables. ♦ Shubel's use of color is highly ordered, with palest blue on the walls, a fresh blue Oxford cloth on sofas, chairs and a daybed, and a richer cornflower blue cotton chenille on an ottoman and pillows. ♦ Shubel draped the windows with very full curtains of white linen. He placed the white curtain rods high on the wall to give them an elegant length and to increase the apparent height of the ceiling.

In the dining room, white-painted Louis XVI–style chairs have seat cushions in periwinkle printed wool/cotton by Bergamo, piped in white denim. The table, which came with the house, was given a glossy coat of auto paint. On a pair of corner plinths, Shubel placed antique Chinese blue-and-white porcelain jars. Lemons and grapefruit on an ironstone platter are from the garden.

Shubel did a complete about-face with the small bedroom overlooking the garden. ◆ "It was a very pokey ten-feet-by-eleven-feet with doors everywhere," he said. ◆ He devised an ingenious way to tent the room in oxford cloth and to disguise the mundane architecture. Metal curtain tracks were affixed around the perimeter of the ceiling. Movable full-length oxford cloth draperies cover all four walls. A piped harlequin valance dressed with white linen tassels conceals the curtain rods and rings, and gives the room a whimsical air. ◆ The daybed is upholstered in Oxford cloth in periwinkle blue, too. A curvy white wing-back chair beside the French doors looks very Alice in Wonderland. ◆ A pair of bleached pine tables, a gift from Silver's mother, stand ready for flowers, books, and cold beverages. ◆ "Steve loved symmetry," said Shubel. Just as the Beach Blanket Babylon producer wished, the decor strikes a balance between perfect polish and effortless ease. It's neat, and quite "done," but hardly intimidating. ◆ Two weeks before he died, Steve Silver and his wife entertained at the cottage, sitting out in the gazebo until the sun set. ◆ "We have always been so happy in the Sonoma house," said Schuman Silver. "Planning the decorating and discussing every aspect of the landscape design gave Steve so much pleasure."

Shubel transformed a former bedroom into a sitting room overlooking the garden. The room had five doors—including French doors, a closet door, and a hall door—so he designed a "tent" of Summer Hill oxford cloth that hangs on ceiling rods. The wall draperies can be closed to conceal the doors and give a more elegant, cohesive feeling. "I wanted the room to feel like a cabana overlooking the pool," said Shubel. The daybed is upholstered in the same cotton Oxford cloth. Pillows are covered in striped cotton fabrics.

Shubel's design for the pool house is at once romantic and very practical. The floor is pink/gray flagstone. The designer chose white terry cloth to cover the bed, all of the wicker chair cushions, the draperies, and the side table skirt. "It feels great on bare skin, and at the end of the weekend, it can all be thrown in the wash," said Shubel.

Bullion fringe on the draperies and skirted table is in jute. The walls and the ceiling were painted cotton candy pink, in homage to designer John Dickinson's original color scheme at the Sonoma Mission Inn. The plaster wine-jug basket lamps with white shades were designed by John Dickinson.

The gazebo offers shelter from the hot Sonoma summer sun. White washed-denim draperies hang from grommets so that they can be removed and cleaned in November for winter storage. Four white-painted wicker chairs have pillows in black and white, with black buttons.

A round wicker table is the perfect position for flowers, books, cool drinks. Roses, geraniums, and lemon trees grow particularly well in the sheltered garden, designed by landscape architect Edward Nicolaus.

DESIGN & STYLE OF THE STATE

BY DIANE DORRANS SAEKS

CALIFORNIA HAS ALWAYS BEEN A STATE OF WHITE-HOT CREATIVITY. HERE ON THE PACIFIC EDGE OF THE CONTINENT, BLUE-SKY IDEAS AND TREND-SETTING STYLES COME TO LIFE. ♦ TALENTED CALIFORNIA ARCHITECTS, INTERIOR DESIGNERS, CRAFTSPEOPLE, FURNITURE AND FABRIC DESIGNERS, STORE OWNERS, ARTISTS, AND PRODUCT DESIGNERS EXPLORE NEW WORLDS, AND CREATE AND OFFER BREAKTHROUGH DESIGNS. ♦ THE FOLLOWING ARE MY FAVORITE WORTH-A-DETOUR STORES, GALLERIES AND HOTELS THROUGHOUT CALIFORNIA. THESE OUTSTANDING SHOPS AND GALLERIES—FROM SANTA MONICA TO MENDOCINO—DICTATE NO ONE STYLE AND FAVOR NO SINGLE DECOR. THEY ARE NOTABLE BECAUSE ONE BRILLIANT, FOCUSED OWNER OR IN-SYNCH PARTNERS (BACKED UP BY A DEDICATED STAFF) HAVE THE IDIOSYNCRATIC MISSION AND ENERGY TO GIVE THEIR COMPANIES A DISTINCT, INSPIRING POINT OF VIEW TO MAKE THEM EVOLVE AND LAST. DESIGN HERE IS LIKE MUSICAL CHAIRS. FOR SOME, THE STYLE IS FULL-TILT BOOGIE-WOOGIE; FOR OTHERS IT'S A SLOW WALTZ.

DESIGN STORES

Los Angeles

AMERICAN RAG CIE, MAISON ET CAFE
148 S. La Brea Avenue
Pick up Provencal pottery, books, tile-top tables, French kitchenware— then sip an espresso at the cafe.

PAMELA BARSKY
100 N. La Cienega Boulevard
(Beverly Connection)
Decorative objects, tabletop decor with fresh style and wit.

BLACKMAN-CRUZ
800 N. La Cienega Blvd
Store partners have a great eye for stylish and odd twentieth-century objects and furniture. A serious favorite with in-the-know design followers.

BOOK SOUP
8818 Sunset Boulevard
West Hollywood
Must-see bookstore, with late closing for midnight browsing. Endless design, architecture, and photography books. Adjacent magazine stand has all the best international design magazines.

CITY ANTIQUES
8444 Melrose Avenue
A fine source for eighteenth- through twentieth-century furniture, some by admired but slightly obscure designers.

NANCY CORZINE
8747 Melrose Avenue
(Open to the trade only.) Superbly edited, suavely updated classic furnishings. Outstanding fabric collection.

DIALOGICA
8304 Melrose Avenue
Smooth contemporary furniture.

DIAMOND FOAM & FABRIC
611 S. La Brea Avenue
Long a secret source for well-priced fabrics, Jason Asch's bustling treasure house offers the added benefit of off-the-rack linen, chintz, silk, and damask shopping.

HOLLYHOCK
214 N. Larchmont Blvd.
Fabrics, furniture, and decorative accessories for house and garden.

INDIGO SEAS
123 N. Robertson Boulevard
Lynn von Kersting's madly inspiring style: part Caribbean Colonial, part South of France, part Old England. Sofas, soaps. Stars come here and buy everything.

LIEF
8922 Beverly Boulevard
Elegant pared-down Gustavian antiques and no-nonsense Scandinavian Biedermeier are a refreshing change from Fine French Furniture. Light and lovely furnishings.

LA MAISON DU BAL
705 N. Harper Avenue
The gracious Bals have gained a following for their exquisite vintage textiles, delicious lighting, antique French furniture. Friendly welcome, great atmosphere.

MODERNICA
7366 Beverly Boulevard
Modernist furniture, focusing on twenties to sixties. Reproductions.

RICHARD MULLIGAN-SUNSET COTTAGE
8157 Sunset Boulevard
(Open to the trade only.) Richard and Mollie have a star-quality following among Hollywood designers and celebs. Antique and vintage country-style antiques. Beautifully finessed painted reproductions and collectible one-of-a-kind lamps.

One-of-a-kind lamp by Richard Mulligan Sunset Cottage, Los Angeles

ODALISQUE
7278 Beverly Boulevard
Best and quirkiest embroidered antique fabrics and glorious vintage textiles. One-of-a-kind pillows and draperies made from ecclesiastical, operatic, and whimsical fabrics. The owners' obsession and admiration of old fabrics has attracted star-power clients.

PACIFIC DESIGN CENTER
8687 Melrose Avenue
To-the-trade showrooms such as Mimi London, Donghia, Randolph & Hein, and Kneedler-Fauchere present the finest fabrics, furniture, lighting, rugs, hardware, reproductions, decorative accessories, fixtures.

RANDY FRANKS
8448 Melrose Place
One-of-a-kind furniture and new designs by young talent.

RIZZOLI BOOKSTORE
9501 Wilshire Boulevard
332 Santa Monica Boulevard, Santa Monica
Top-notch selection of design and architecture books.

ROSE TARLOW — MELROSE HOUSE
8454 Melrose Place
Rose Tarlow has a great sense of furniture scale and an exquisite understanding of line and grace. A certain English sensibility and glamour in her furniture collection.

RUSSELL SIMPSON COMPANY
8109 Melrose Avenue
Bret Witke and Diane Rosenstein sell furniture from the forties and fifties. Eames, Jacobsen, Saarinen, Robsjohn-Gibbings.

San Francisco

AD/50
Corner Laguna & Hayes Streets
Dominic Longacre is a passionate collector and purveyor of mid-century furniture by architects. In addition to chairs, tables, and storage systems by the likes of the Eameses and George Nelson, he offers new modernist furniture designs by Park Furniture, based in San Francisco.

AGRARIA
1051 Howard Street
Maurice Gibson and Stanford Stevenson's elegant potpourri and soaps are tops. A chic (and very fragrant) store. (By appointment only: 415-863-7700.)

ARCH
407 Jackson Street
Architect Susan Colliver's graphic store sells supplies for designers, architects, and artists. Fun place. Excellent range of papers, pencils, frames.

Pleated silk napkin by Ann Gish, Newberry Park

BELL'OCCHIO
8 Brady Street
Claudia Schwartz and Toby Hanson's whimsical boutique offers hand-painted ribbons, French silk flowers, charming tableware, antiques, and wonderfully retro Italian and Parisian powders.

BLOOMERS
2975 Washington Street
Under Patric Powell's sure and stylish guidance, fragrant Bloomers blooms year-round with delicious cut flowers, orchids, bulbs, vases, French ribbons, and baskets. Phone with confidence to order a thrilling flower arrangement.
.
VIRGINIA BREIER
3091 Sacramento Street
A gallery for contemporary and traditional American crafts, including furniture and tableware.

BRITEX
146 Geary Street
Action central for thousands of fabrics. World-class selections of classic and unusual furnishing textiles. (Don't forget to rummage among the rich remnants.)

BROWN DIRT COWBOYS
2418 Polk Street
Painted and refurbished furniture, housewares.

CANDELIER
60 Maiden Lane
Wade Bentson's harmonious ballad to the candle and its accoutrements. Superb collection of candlesticks and tabletop decor.

COLUMBINE DESIGN
1541 Grant Avenue
Kathleen Dooley sells flowers, dried blossoms (in Victorian and Mexican styles), along with shells, framed butterflies, and beetles.

THE COTTAGE TABLE COMPANY
550 18th Street
An architects' and designers' favorite. Congenial old-world craftsman Tony Cowan, serious about traditional fine tables, custom makes heirloom-quality classic hardwood tables to order. A rare find. Shipping available. Catalogue.

EARTHSAKE
2076 Chestnut Street
(also in Palo Alto and Berkeley)
Charming earth-friendly store selling attractive unbleached bed linens and towels, politically correct beds, glasses and vases of recycled glass, candles,

DE VERA
334 Gough Street
Objets trouves, fine art, sculpture. Remarkable, original small-scale finds by Federico de Vera.

DE VERA GLASS
384 Hayes Street
A rigorously edited gallery of vibrant glass objects by contemporary American artists, along with Venetian and Scandinavian classics.

F. DORIAN
388 Hayes Street
Contemporary accessories, folk arts, and antiques.

FILLAMENTO
2185 Fillmore Street
Mecca for design aficionados. Owner
Iris Fuller orchestrates three floors of
well-modulated style-conscious furniture, tableware, toiletries, and gifts.
Iris is always first with new designers'
works and supports local talent
including Annieglass and Cyclamen
Studio tabletop decor. Frames, lamps,
linens, beds, and partyware.

FIORIDELLA
1920 Polk Street
Jean Thompson and Barbara Belloli
sell the most luscious flowers in a
store full of sensual, fragrant blooms
and plants. International selection of
decorative and versatile vases. Phone
for deliveries of beautiful arrangements for special occasions.

FLAX
1699 Market Street
Vast and tasty selections of papers,
lighting, tabletop accessories, boxes,
art books, furnishings. Action central
for art supplies. Catalogue.

GALLERIA DESIGN CENTER
101 Henry Adams Street
This to-the-trade-only building—
along with the Showplace Design
Center, Showplace West, and other
nearby showrooms—offers top-of-
the-line furniture, fabrics, and
furnishings. Randolph & Hein,
Kneedler-Fauchere, Sloan Miyasato,
Shears & Window, Donghia, Summit
Furniture, Clarence House, Enid
Ford, and Houles are personal
favorites. Also in the neighborhood:
Therien & Co. (Scandinavian,
Continental and English antiques,
and Therien Studio reproductions)
and the handsome outpost of
Ed Hardy San Francisco (eclectic
antiques and reproductions).

STANLEE R. GATTI FLOWERS
Fairmont Hotel, Nob Hill
Beautiful flowers, Agraria potpourri,
Zinc Details monkeytail glass vases,
and candles.

GREEN WORLD MERCANTILE
2340 Polk Street
Altruistic owners have carved a niche
for themselves selling earth-friendly
housewares, clothing, gardening
equipment, a pleasing range of decorative accessories.

GUMP'S
135 Post Street
A treasure chest of fine art and
Orient-inspired accessories, plus timeless furniture and elegant tableware.
Recent refurbishing makes the store
(open since 1861) an essential stop.
Be sure to visit the silver, jewelry,
stationery, Treillage, and decorative
glass departments. Catalogue.

RICHARD HILKERT BOOKS
333 Hayes Street
Bibliophiles, music lovers, decorators,
and antiquarians telephone Richard
to order out-of-print style books and
seek out newest design books. When
you visit Hilkert's store, it's like
entering the study of a cozy friend.

INDIGO V
1352 Castro Street
Diane's fresh flowers are never ordi-
nary. A city-wide favorite.

JAPONESQUE
824 Montgomery Street
Koichi Hara celebrates the Japanese
love of tradition, harmony, simplicity,
refined beauty, humble materials.
Graphics, sculpture, glass, furniture.
The spirit of his design gallery is
entirely timeless and transcendent.

KRIS KELLY
1 Union Square
Fine selections of bed and table
linens.

LIMN
290 Townsend Street
Contemporary furniture and lighting
by over 300 manufacturers. Philippe
Starck to Le Corbusier and Andree
Putman and Mathieu & Ray, along
with Northern California talent.

Gump's, San Francisco

MAC (Satellite of Love)
5 Claude Lane
Ben Ospital's domain: witty housewares, furnishings, and modern,
appealing clothing in charming style-
filled Claude Lane. (And to keep it
all in the family, trip out to Chris
Ospital's MAC, 1543 Grant Ave, for
style inspiration.)

MACY'S
Union Square
The furniture and decorative accessories floors display a vast selection
of furnishings. The Interior Design
Department has designers available to
assist with decorating. New: Calvin
Klein Home. Macy's is a lively
marketplace also offering tableware,
kitchenware and kitchen tools.

MIKE FURNITURE
Corner Fillmore & Sacramento St.
With design directed by Mike Moore
and his partner Mike Thackar, this
spacious, sunny store sells updated
furniture classics-with-a-twist by
Beverly and other manufacturers.
They make forward design very accessible. One-stop shopping for fast-
delivery sofas, fabrics, lamps, tables,
fabrics, accessories.

NAOMI'S ANTIQUES TO GO
1817 Polk Street
Art pottery to the rafters! Bauer and
Fiesta, of course, plus historic studio
pottery, American railroad, airline,
luxury liner, and bus depot china.

NEST
2300 Fillmore Street
In the Victorian building where a
beloved pharmacy stood for decades,
Marcella Madsen and Judith Gilman
have feathered a new Nest. Sweet silk
flowers, rustic antiques, prints,
sachets, and books are their forte.

PAINT EFFECTS
2426 Fillmore Street
Paint enthusiasts and experts, Sheila
Rauch and her partner Patricia
Orlando have a dedicated following
selling a wide range of innovative
paint finishes. Excellent, hands-on
paint technique classes are offered,
along with materials for gilding,
liming, crackle glazing, decoupage,
stenciling, and many other decorative
finishes.

PAXTON GATE
1204 Stevenson Street
Peter Kline and Sean Quigley's gardening store sells uncommon plants
(such as sweetly scented Buddha's
Hand citron trees) along with local
artists' works, orchids, vases, and
hand-forged tools.

POLANCO
393 Hayes Street
Colorful, superbly presented Mexican
arts, photography, and crafts.
Museum curator Elsa Cameron says
you won't find better in Mexico City.

PORTOBELLO
3915 24th Street
A tiny treasure. Old furniture in new
guises, kilims, decorative objects.

POTTERY BARN
The San Francisco-based company
has stores all over California. New
full-service design stores offer furniture, rugs, draperies, special orders.
Great, practical home style at a price.
Excellent basics. Ever-changing, accessible, easy-to-love design. Catalogue.

RAYON VERT
3187 16th Street
Kelly Kornegay's garden of earthly delights! Flowers, artifacts, glasses, architectural fragments in a stylish, operatic setting. Worth the trip to the Mission district.

RH
2506 Sacramento Street
Rick Herbert's lovely garden and tableware store has dramatically displayed candles, dinnerware by Sebastapol artist Aletha Soule. Inspiring selection of books, cachepots, vases. Topiaries, too.

RIZZOLI BOOKSTORE
117 Post Street
Top-notch selection of design and architecture books.

SATIN MOON FABRICS
32 Clement Street
Twenty-two-year-old store sells a well-edited collection of decorating linens, chintzes and well-priced fabrics.

SCHEUER LINENS
340 Sutter Street
Long-time favorite store for fine-quality bed linens, blankets. This store handles custom orders particularly well.

SHABBY CHIC
3075 Sacramento Street
Specializes in chairs and sofas with comfortable airs and loose-fitting slipcovers.

SLIPS
1534 Grant Avenue
Sami Rosenzweig's on-the-go, innovative shop sells and custom-makes slipcovers for chairs and sofas, plus draperies, decorations, ottomans. Sami has a million ideas for improving furniture with slipcovers—all cost-conscious and stylish.

SUE FISHER KING
3067 Sacramento Street
Sue King's Italian and French linens and tableware are the finest and prettiest. A must-stop shop for chic accessories and gifts, books, soaps, furniture, and luxurious throws.

SUE FISHER KING AT WILKES BASHFORD
375 Sutter Street
Sue's vision blazes here with tableware, accessories, furniture, and special *objets d'art* from Italy, France, England.

WILLIAMS-SONOMA
150 Post Street
Flagship for the Williams Sonoma cookware empire. Stores throughout the state, including Corte Madera, Palo Alto, Rodeo Drive, Pasadena. Delicacies. Outstanding basics for serious and dilettante cooks. Catalogues.

WILLIAM STOUT ARCHITECTURAL BOOKS
804 Montgomery Street
Architect Bill Stout's chock-a-block store specialises in basic and obscure twentieth-century architecture publications, along with new and out-of-print design books. Catalogues.

WORLDWARE
336 Hayes Street
Shari Sant's stylish eco-store sells cosy unbleached sheets and blankets, vintage-wear, clean-lined clothing for men and women, and such delights as patchwork pillows, deluxe soaps. Interiors crafted by Dan Plummer from recycled materials are very handsome. Catalogue.

ZINC DETAILS
1905 Fillmore Street
The Zinc shop has a cult following. Architect-designed and handcrafted furniture, lighting. Extraordinary hand-blown glass vases by local artists. Provocative, special domain of Wendy Nishimura and Vasilios Kiniris.

ZONAL HOME INTERIORS
568 Hayes Street
Russell Pritchard's pioneering gallery store of one-of-a-kind rustic furniture and decorative objects, most with the patina of rust and the textures of loving use. This is Americana at its best.

Berkeley

Much of the design store action here is focused on wonderfully revived Fourth Street. We recommend, too, a detour to Cafe Fanny, the Acme Bread bakery, Chez Panisse, and shops in the Elmwood.

BERKELEY MILLS
2830 Seventh Street
Much-admired crafting of furniture and furnishings. Japanese- and Mission-influenced furniture. Blends the best of old-world craftsmanship with high-tech. All built to order. Catalogue.

BUILDERS BOOKSOURCE
1817 Fourth Street
Excellent design, architecture, gardening, and building book source.

CAMPS AND COTTAGES
2109 Virginia Street
Lunch at Chez Panisse or Berkeley's beloved Cheese Board, then skip here for a visit. This sprightly and well-stocked little shop sells charming homey furniture and low-key accessories. Owner Molly Hyde English has perfect pitch for the nineties.

CYCLAMEN STUDIO
1825 Eastshore Highway
Julie Sanders's colorful ceramics seconds—with barely discernible flaws —are available at the factory by appointment. (Her vibrant and very collectible Cyclamen Studio designs are featured at Fillamento.) The hot-off-the-kiln Re-Eco line, new ceramics made of ground-up, recycled old ceramics, is very innovative.

Ken Probst

Maison d'Etre

EARTHSAKE
1805 Fourth Street
One of the pioneers in environmentally safe household goods, this charming store dishes it all up with great panache. It's also a fine place to gain an education in what's good for the planet.

THE GARDENER
1836 Fourth Street
Alta Tingle's brilliant, inspired store sells tools, vases, books, tables, chairs, tableware, paintings, clothing, and food for garden lovers—whether they have a garden or are just dreaming. Consistently original style.

LIGHTING STUDIO
1808 Fourth Street
Lighting design services. Contemporary lamps.

TAIL OF THE YAK
2632 Ashby Avenue
Partners Alice Hoffman Erb and Lauren Adams Allard have created an entrancing store that is always a treat. Absolutely worth the drive to this quiet Elmwood neighborhood. Decorative accessories, Mexican furniture, fabrics, ribbons, notecards, Lauren's books, tableware, and antique jewelry.

ERICA TANOV
1627 San Pablo Avenue
Erica's lace-edged sheets and shams, and linen duvet covers are chic and quietly luxurious. (Pop into Kermit Lynch Wine Merchants, Acme Bread, and Cafe Fanny just up the street.)

ZIA
1310 Tenth Street
Collin Smith's sun-filled gallery-store offers a changing variety of hands-on furniture designs and art.

Big Sur

THE PHOENIX
Highway One
An enduring favorite store. Splendid collections of handcrafted decorative objects, glass, books, sculpture, jewelry, hand-knit sweaters by Kaffe Fassett (who grew up in Big Sur), and toys. Extraordinary coastal views from the windows. Be sure to visit the downstairs boutiques. Crystal, soothing music, and hand-made objects are on all sides. The sixties never left Big Sur—thank goodness.

Burlingame

GARDENHOUSE
1129 Howard Avenue
Topiaries, garden ornaments, beautifully presented decorative accessories.

Carmel

CARMEL BAY COMPANY
Corner of Ocean & Lincoln
Tableware, books, glassware, furniture, prints.

LUCIANO ANTIQUES
San Carlos and Fifth Streets
Wander through the vast rooms to view cosmopolitan antiques and handsome reproductions from everywhere, every time period.

Healdsburg

JIMTOWN STORE
6706 State Highway 128
J. Carrie Brown and John Werner's friendly country store in the Alexander Valley. Be sure to visit their Mercantile & Exchange. Vintage Americana is cheerful and very well-priced.

PALLADIO
324 Healdsburg Avenue
Tom Scheibal worked with architect Andrew Jaszewski to create a spectacular, sunny design store. Chairs, tables, armoires with a country air. When in Healdsburg, also discover The Raven movie theater, Ravenous restaurant, and new shops around the historic square.

Mendocino

THE GOLDEN GOOSE
Main Street
Superior embellished linens, antiques, tableware, overlooking the ocean. For more than a decade, the most stylish store in Mendocino. (When in Mendocino, be sure to make a dinner reservation at Cafe Beaujolais and visit Wilkes Sport.)

Mill Valley

CAPRICORN ANTIQUES & COOKWARE
100 Throckmorton Avenue
This solid, reliable store seems to have been on this corner forever. Excellent, basic cookware, along with antique tables, chests, and cupboards.

PULLMAN & CO.
108 Throckmorton Avenue
Understated but luxurious bed linens (the standouts are those by Ann Gish), along with furniture, frames, tableware, and accessories.

Paper White linens by Jan Dutton

SMITH & HAWKEN
35 Corte Madera
First visit the nursery (begun under horticulturist Sarah Hammond's superb direction) and then the store. Everything for gardens. Also in Berkeley, Palo Alto, Los Gatos, Santa Rosa, and points beyond. Outstanding catalogues.

SUMMER HOUSE GALLERY
21 Throckmorton Avenue
Artist-crafted accessories and excellent, comfortable sofas and chairs. Witty handcrafted frames, glassware, candlesticks, and colorful accessories. Slipcovered loveseats, vases, tables, gifts.

Montecito

PIERRE LAFOND/ WENDY FOSTER
516 San Ysidro Road
Handsomely displayed household furnishings, books, accessories and South American and Malabar Coast furniture. Beautiful linens.

Oakland

MAISON D'ETRE
5330 College Avenue
Indoor/outdoor style. Engaging, eccentric, and whimsical decorative objects and furniture for rooms and gardens. (Look for their newest store in South Park, San Francisco.)

Palo Alto

BELL'S BOOKS
536 Emerson Street
An especially fine and thorough selection of new, vintage, and rare books on every aspect of gardens and gardening. Also literature, books on decorative arts, scholarly volumes.

HILLARY THATZ
Stanford Shopping Center
A singular, embellished view of the interiors of England, as seen by Cheryl Driver. Accessories, furniture, frames, and decorative objects. Beautifully presented garden furnishings.

POLO/RALPH LAUREN
Stanford Shopping Center
A handsome, gracious store. A world through Ralph Lauren's Anglophile eyes. Outstanding selection of furniture, imaginary heritage accessories, and quality housewares. Catalogue.

TURNER MARTIN
540 Emerson Street
David Turner and John Martin's enchanting one-of-a-kind style store/gallery. Definitely worth a detour for their displays of frames, lighting, books, tables, photographs by David, vases, and chairs, occasionally with fresh-grass seats.

Palm ceramics at Summer House Gallery

Pasadena

HORTUS
284 E. Orange Grove Boulevard
Superbly selected perennials, antique roses, and a full nursery. Handsome collection of antique garden ornaments.

San Anselmo

MODERN i
500 Red Hill Avenue
Steven Cabella is passionate about Modernism and time-warp mid-century (1935-65) furnishings. Vintage furnishings, Eames chairs, furniture by architects, objects, and artwork. Located in a restored modernist architect's office building.

San Rafael

MANDERLEY
Ronnie Wells's full-tilt glamorous silk shams, antique fabrics, and vintage pillows set trends. Outstanding throws in one-of-a-kind textiles. (By appointment only: 415.472.6166.)

St. Helena

BALE MILL CLASSIC COUNTRY FURNITURE
3431 North St. Helena Highway
Decorative and practical updated classic furniture in a wide range of styles. A favorite with decorators.

MOSSWOOD
1239 Main Street
Garden style. An elegant collection of birdhouses, handpainted case clocks, garden ornaments and garden tools.

ST. HELENA ST. HELENA ANTIQUES
1231 Main Street
(Yes, the name is intentionally repetitious.) Rustic vintage wine paraphernalia, vintage furniture.

Annieglass Designs

TANTAU
1220 Adams Street
Decorative accessories, handpainted furniture, gifts.

TESORO
649 Main Street
Fresh-flower heaven. Topiaries, wreaths, vases, too.

TIVOLI
1432 Main Street
Tom Scheibal and partners have created another winner, an indoor/outdoor garden furniture and accessories store. Tables and chairs and useful occasional pieces are in iron, aluminum, concrete, and recycled redwood. Antique garden ornaments.

VANDERBILT & CO.
1429 Main Street
Stylish and colorful tableware, bed linens, books, glassware, Italian ceramics, accessories. A year-round favorite in the wine country.

Santa Monica

THOMAS CALLAWAY BENCHWORKS, INC.
2920 Nebraska Avenue
Interior designer Thomas Callaway crafts custom arm chairs, sofas, and ottomans with deep-down comfort and real glamour. These are future heirlooms, very collectible. (By appointment only: 310.828.9379).

HENNESSY & INGALLS
1254 Third Street, Promenade
Architects and designers gravitate to this book store, which specializes in the widest range of architectural books.

IRELAND-PAYS
2428 Main Street
Producer Kathryn Ireland and actress Amanda Pays (*Max Headroom*) created *le style anglais* for Anglophile Angelenos. Special pillows.

JASPER
1454 Fifth Street
Interior designer Michael Smith's brilliant store and atelier. In a grand former art gallery, the high-ceilinged shop displays changing vignettes of antiques, linens, cashmeres, art glass, and Smith's own designs. Worth a detour.

ROOM WITH A VIEW
1600 Montana Avenue
Kitchenware, children's furnishings, and especially glamorous bed linens by Cocoon (silks), Bischoff, and Anichini.

SHABBY CHIC
1013 Montana Avenue
Yes, they still do great smooshy sofas, but they've also moved on to tailored upholstery and a new line of fabrics.

Sonoma

SLOAN AND JONES
147 E. Spain Street
Ann Jones and Sheelagh Sloan just opened this splendid antiques and tableware store. Set in a fine old turn-of-the-century building, it's Action Central for country and Asian vintage furniture, photography, linens, and garden accessories.

THE SONOMA COUNTRY STORE
165 West Napa Street
Ann Thornton's empire also includes her store at 3575 Sacramento Street, San Francisco. Decorative accessories, linens. Great for Christmas decorations and gifts.

Venice

BOUNTIFUL
1335 Abbott Kinney Boulevard
Great Edwardian and Victorian painted furniture, lamps, old beds, quirky *objets*. (By appointment only: 310.450.3620.)

Penina Meisels

Nikolas Weinstein

FLEA MARKETS

Another way to see design in action is to go flea-marketing at California antiques and collectibles markets. The Long Beach, Pasadena Rose Bowl, and San Francisco fleas are tops. See newspaper listings for dates of special antiques shows, swap meets, fairs, and markets. (Insider tip: Go early.)

HOTELS

City & Country

A view outside your window—especially if it includes a pool, a valley, Pacific surf, or a bougainvillea bower—is a must. These chic award-winning hotels afford an only-in-California visit. All well-placed—overlooking San Francisco Bay, on the Carmel coast, high on spectacular hills, or in beautifully designed gardens—each hotel offers a cosseted vantage point.

AUBERGE DU SOLEIL
180 Rutherford Hill Road
Rutherford ♦ 707.963.1211
Respected hotelier and restaurateur Claude Rouas worked with architect Sandy Walker and designer Michael Taylor to create a chic, sunny wine country hotel. Outstanding cuisine, heart-stopping hillside views of the Napa Valley from the restaurant terraces and rooms.

HOTEL BEL-AIR
701 Stone Canyon Road
Los Angeles ♦ 310.472.1211
Glamorous and suavely low-key, the Bel-Air is unlike any other hotel. Often called the best hotel in the world, it's beloved for its luxurious garden setting, the sunny and very private suites, and helpful staff. Not to be missed: Breakfast on the loggia, walks in the canyon, lunch beside the oval swimming pool, and a romantic dinner overlooking the swan lake. The silence here is solace after the stresses of Los Angeles.

HUNTINGTON HOTEL
1075 California Street
San Francisco ♦ 415.474.5400
On the crown of Nob Hill overlooking Huntington Park, this hotel has a handsome presence. For residents and visitors alike, it's a San Francisco treasure. The clanging and clanking sounds of the cable cars are background music to the English-style rooms.

Mary Nichols

Hotel Bel-Air

THE LODGE AT PEBBLE BEACH
17-Mile Drive
Pebble Beach ♦ 408.624.3811
Simply one of the most beautiful hotel settings in the world. Play golf, sunbathe at the Beach and Tennis Club, or drive down to Big Sur for the day.

MEADOWOOD RESORT
900 Meadowood Lane
St Helena ♦ 707.963.3646
Like reposing on your own leafy estate in the Napa Valley. Quiet, understated suites among the oak trees. Croquet, hiking, tennis, golf—or just reading on a quiet verandah. Within minutes of St. Helena, dozens of wineries, the spectacular valley.

HOTEL MONACO
Corner Geary Boulevard & Taylor Street
San Francisco ♦ 415.292.0100
In a handsome renovated 1910 Beaux Arts building, the Monaco feels like an international crossroads. Los Angeles designer Cheryl Rowley decorated the rooms.

The Lodge at Pebble Beach

POST RANCH INN
Highway One
Big Sur ♦ 408.667.2200
Cliff-side environmentally correct hotel designed by Mickey Muennig. Stands along an unseen ridge on the edge of the Pacific, on 36 wild acres. Just thirty rooms. Musts: hiking trails, swimming, exploring the neighboring national parks—and gazing out to sea.

PRESCOTT HOTEL
545 Post Street
San Francisco ♦ 415.563.0303
Interiors designed by San Francisco designer Nan Rosenblatt. Club Level has a concierge, evening refreshments, morning breakfast in a private lounge. Best of all: room service from Wolfgang Puck's Postrio downstairs.

RITZ-CARLTON HOTEL
600 Stockton Street at California Street
San Francisco ♦ 415.296.7464
Glorious views over San Francisco. Like all Ritz-Carlton hotels, this superbly run hotel offers cosseting and comfort. Afternoon tea is served daily in the lobby lounge. Be sure to visit the spa and indoor pool—especially in the evening.

RITZ-CARLTON LAGUNA NIGUEL
33533 Ritz-Carlton Drive
Dana Point ♦ 714.240.2000
Splendid, shining location overlooking the Pacific Ocean and near some of the best surfing beaches in Southern California. Rooms open to sea breezes, sunsets. Two swimming pools and paths down to the beach.

SAN YSIDRO RANCH
900 San Ysidro Lane
Montecito ♦ 805.969.5046
Privacy seekers and worldly guests who love its warm, homey style return to the Ranch year after year. The ranch property was originally a land grant from the King of Spain to Franciscan friars, who ran cattle there. Hillside rooms in vibrant gardens.

SHERMAN HOUSE
2160 Green Street
San Francisco ♦ 415.563.3600
A historic Pacific Heights mansion superbly converted into a highly civilized hotel. Rooms were designed by Billy Gaylord. Hollywood stars and business leaders appreciate its privacy, discretion, and attention to detail. Unobtrusively well-managed. Quiet gardens, fine restaurant. Convenient location near Union Street. (Plumpjack Cafe designed by Leavitt/Weaver is just along Fillmore Street.)

HOTEL TRITON
342 Grant Avenue
San Francisco ♦ 415.394.0500
Overlooks the gates of San Francisco's Chinatown. With its downtown location and witty interiors designed by San Francisco's Michael Moore, this hotel is a favorite with cool internationals. Be sure to sit in the lobby's Diva chair, by Goodman Charlton. (Ask about the suite designed by boxer shorts mogul Joe Boxer.)

VENTANA INN RESORT
Highway One
Big Sur ♦ 408.667.2331
With understated (and now weathered) buildings originally designed by Kipp Stewart, Ventana stands high and mighty in the hills. Restaurant terrace has a dazzling view of Big Sur and the Pacific Ocean. A wonderful base for hiking, swimming, watching the fog roll over the coast — and solitude and privacy.

John Vaughan

Hotel Monaco